Live

Laugh

Fly

***A Family's Journey Through Childhood Cancer,
Unimaginable Grief,
and the Realization that Love Never Dies***

Christina McMurray

Eugene McMurray

1

I experienced the tragedy of Scott's death. Thanks to Chris and Gene I am now blessed to have experienced his amazing life. What an extraordinary and loving young man he was.

SANDEE " Candy" Martensen
Founder/Exec Dir - The Pinwheel Project

This is a book and journey about the language of the heart. A must read especially in this time of Covid 19.

Cheryl Burton RN, Hospice of Westchester

Live – Laugh - Fly offers the reader an opportunity to dig deeply into the mysteries of life. You will cry, laugh, and be transformed. A must read for all.

Laura Corsun, Founder of High and Mighty
A therapeutic riding and driving equine center

Day after day as I watched the McMurrays navigate their unthinkable journey, I was amazed at their poise and Grace. Chris, Gene, and Kim cared for Scott with endless love and Scott, in turn, showed wisdom beyond his years. When it was time to say Goodbye, they left nothing undone, nothing unsaid.

Dr. Beverly Thornhill, Montefiore Medical Center

Here is a rich portrait of how faith, perseverance, forgiveness, and hope carried this family through the illness and death of a remarkable son/brother from rare cancer. It concludes with an encouraging testimony about life after life.

Bruce Page, Retired Presbyterian minister and Hospice worker chaplaincy, bereavement counselor, volunteer coordinator

"This will not be a sad house". Yes, this. We are each responsible for how we respond to crises. There can be joy during devastation and peace in times of turmoil. I believed in this before I met Scott, Chris, and Gene. Now, after having been honored to accompany them in Scott's end of life journey, I have proof. This is more than a memorial, a tribute, or a window into the world of the McMurray family. This is a road map for families who need to learn how to reframe tragedy; how to truly squeeze the life out of every day. Scott's and his parents grace has become the beacon I use to help other families who also face their child's end of life. Thank you for the lessons you have taught me and for helping me become a better social worker.

Denise Velazquez LCSW, Children's Hospital @ Montefiore

The McMurrays will touch your heart like no other and inspire you to walk in God's footsteps with Grace in the midst of pain, anger, acceptance, forgiveness, love, gratitude and belief. Scott will inspire you to LIVE LIFE TO THE FULLEST. Forever stamped on my heart.

Sandy V Marques BSN RN

A deeply moving story of how one couple navigates life while coming to terms with their son's terminal illness. A story that shows how strength and peace can be born from love, even during the most unimaginable parental nightmare.

Eileen Flagg

DEDICATION

In loving memory of

Scott McMurray

November 29, 1988

April 27, 2011

He showed us how to live

He helped us all to laugh

And today, he flies with the angels.

For all the moms and dads, sisters and brothers, who face this same challenge, we hope that Scott's story reminds you that love is forever.

ACKNOWLEDGEMENTS

First, I want to Thank my son Scott for nudging me to write this story. It was hard, the reminders were so painful, but now I can say that I am glad I did it. You have shown me so much love and I couldn't be prouder! Keep laughing, keep flying! We will see each other again, this I know for sure. So happy you are mine!

To my husband Gene: What a wild ride it has been. You are my love and one of my favorite people. Your trust and unconditional love is something I will never take for granted. We have literally been thru it all and can still find the humor and always know that together there is nothing we can't do. Maybe I'm Amazed.

To my daughter Kim: Because of you I am a Mom. This is my favorite part of my life. Because of you I wanted to do better, I wanted to be better. Your love, kindness and compassion make the world a better place. I am so proud of you. So happy you are mine! To Eileen and Barbara: By chance we became sisters in law, by choice we became sisters. Thank you for this gift!

Barbara: Thank you for your wisdom, encouragement, and many hours of your editing skills. Some days were not easy but look! We did it!

Eileen: Thank you for your compassion, your empathy and your amazing ability to know just what to do in any situation, I am so grateful that you are Scott's godmother.

To Jim, Kathryn, Mike and Megan: I couldn't ask for better cousins for Kim and Scott. You are always there for each other and I am so proud of each of you.

To Lori, Susan, Eileen F, Laura and Donna: Thank you for continuing to push me when I wanted to give up writing this book. Thank you for remembering stories when I had forgotten, and Thanks for the belly laughs and the shoulders to cry on when I needed.

To my New York friends: I am so nervous that I would leave someone out so let me say Thank you. Thank you for the love and kindness you showed my family. Thank you for the hugs. You were with us and we know and appreciate that.

To Hitchcock Presbyterian Church: Thank you for lifting us up. Your cards, meals, flowers and calls were a constant support for us. We never felt alone, we felt loved. It is exactly what Jesus would have done.

To Children's Hospital @ Montefiore: You are all so amazing! I do not know how you do it. Not only do you care for our children but you were there for the parents too. You truly are doing God's work and we are forever grateful.

To Hospice of Westchester: Thank you for helping us during Scott's final months. Cheryl, we appreciate all you did for Scott and us. He was surrounded in love from his family and friends. Most importantly, he got to do it his way, how amazing.

Sky Dive the Ranch: Thank you for teaching Scott to Fly and for finding his smile, it was a game changer.

Contents

Foreword

My family is fond of quoting The Beatles. "Take a sad song," we say, "and make it better." I like to think that's what this book is—taking a sad song, the saddest song, and making it a little bit better. This is a book about my brother who died from a rare cancer when he was only 22. It is also about how he is still with us these many years later.

Scott was the most interesting person I ever knew. He was funny, spontaneous and brave. His antics always created the best stories. When he was six, he fell out of our upstairs bathroom window during a blizzard, in his underwear, because he had dropped his lucky pencil. When he was nine, he convinced me, and some friends, that we should have a water gun fight—only, instead of water, we used ketchup and Hershey syrup, and we battled in our kitchen. To this day, it was one of the most fun afternoons of my life.

When Scott was 19, he was diagnosed with desmoplastic small round cell tumor, an aggressive pediatric cancer. He was funny, spontaneous and brave up until the end. And he even managed to cram in some pretty cool stories about jumping out of planes. I would give anything to hear him laugh again.

This is also a book about my parents and how they took the saddest song in the world and made it a little better, a little more manageable, breathable.

My mom is larger than life. When she tells stories (and she tells them often), she uses her whole body and will frequently make me get up and help her act out her anecdotes. She gives a ton of advice about life, love and the best cereal combinations. While it pains me to say it, she is usually right.

She is a force to be reckoned with. When I was young, she went to battle with the Girl Scouts over their father-daughter dance and got it changed to be more inclusive. She ran her own business for 20 years and helped raise more than 100 kids. When Scott got sick, she took care of him completely, from driving to doctor's appointments to making countless milk shakes and grilled cheese sandwiches whenever he could eat. She even wrote an entire book based on a conversation she had with a stranger on a plane.

My dad is more like me, quiet and thoughtful. Even though he doesn't want to, he will get up when my mom asks him to act out a story he has heard a million times. He is a rock. After Scott's first diagnosis, my dad got in the car, turned around to my brother and me and said, "We are going to fight this, as hard as we can, I promise." And he did, until my brother didn't want to fight anymore, and then he let go. (Although, he did once bring in some water blessed by the Pope and sprinkled it on Scott when he wasn't looking.)

He takes care of my mom and me, and I am thankful every day that we have him.

Scott once asked me what happens after we die. We were laying on his bed watching a movie, like we did more and more as he got closer to the end. I wanted to answer him as honestly as I could.

"I don't know. But I know that no matter what, even if you are just gone and everything is dark, you won't be in pain anymore."

Scott thought about this, contemplating my words as Spinal Tap played in the background. "Yeah, I guess so," he said. "But I hope there is a heaven."

"Me too, Scott."

—Kim

Prologue – Stranger On a Plane
2013 - Chris

I was boarding an early morning flight from Charleston to Philadelphia when I made an unexpected connection. When I reached my row, a woman who appeared to be my age, with light brown hair and blue eyes but fewer wrinkles than I, was already seated next to the window. We made eye contact and smiled as I took my seat on the aisle.

We exchanged sleepy pleasantries and talked about the purpose of our flights. I was headed to upstate New York to help a friend with her therapeutic horseback riding camp and annual fundraiser. She was going to some sort of work conference in Maine. She explained that in addition to being a registered nurse, she was trained in energy healing and that she would be attending seminars and classes on the subject. We launched into the usual small talk, exchanging names and learning more details about each other's lives. Her name was Diana and she lived in Summerville, South Carolina. I explained that my husband, Gene, and I were spending the summer in our new condo in Mt. Pleasant, South Carolina.

Then she asked me if I had any children. This is always a difficult question for me and I struggled with the answer. My son, Scott, died at the age of 22. He was diagnosed with a rare cancer called desmoplastic small round cell tumor (DSRCT) when he was just 19 years old. I was aware that if I shared this personal information, it might make her uncomfortable, and we still had an hour left on this flight. However, if I did not mention Scott and only mentioned my daughter Kim, I'd feel like I was betraying him. Each time I share his story, I feel a little bit of the pain again—the grief that never goes away. I decided to tell her. I figured that I would never see her again, so I went for it.

"Yes," I answered, "I have a daughter who lives and works in Washington, DC, and I had a son who passed away two years ago." She turned and looked me straight in the eye.

"Are you a writer?" she asked. "Was your son a writer?"

Confused by her reaction to my sad declaration, I shook my head. But she persisted and continued to ask me about writing. At that point, I really did not know where she was going with this questioning. Why was she so focused on writing? Usually, when I said my son died, people nodded their heads and changed the subject. Then she told me that she was "gifted". I truly had no idea where she was going with all of this.

She went on to say that Scott was speaking to her, that he was telling her he had sent me many signs to let me know that I was supposed to be writing to help other parents with their grieving. As she spoke, her eyes were open, but she paused often to listen and nod her head. At first I was a little nervous, but also excited. My son always kept me hopping, and now, even years after his death, he still was! I had watched *Long Island Medium* on television and hoped that I would run into Theresa Caputo.

"So, he's making work for me," I said, half serious, half joking.

She smiled and nodded. I was now paying attention to this message from Scott. She explained that he was using a phrase not commonly used in the South, "I got your back, Mom. I got your back." My heart skipped a beat, and I lost my breath as tears filled my eyes. Scott always said that.

One of the last times I remember Scott saying this was during his final stages of cancer. We were both laying on his bed listening to The Beatles. He was unable to walk and he was using the oxygen machine 24 hours a day. When he spoke, it was labored. I told him how much I was going to miss him. I then asked him if he would watch over me. He nodded.

"I got your back, Mom," he said, then quickly added, "but not all the time."

"Yeah, not all the time," I said, smiling. "That would be weird."

I laugh when I think of this conversation. That was Scott.

The sound of Diana's voice brought me back to the present. She asked me if I was planning a trip to the mountains – after I said no, she communicated that Scott was referencing Ashville or Nashville. That reminded me of a trip planned for later that summer to Nashville to celebrate Gene's 60th birthday. She then said that Scott was showing her a sign for a bridge – on that bridge he saw me on one end and his dad on the other. He was reminding us that we are to stay in the middle of that bridge. I understood that completely. Knowing that he was dying, Scott told us that we could not become a statistic, as so many parents who lose a child separate or divorce – that we had to stay together.

Then, "He's hugging a dog," she said.

I looked at her, tears falling down my cheeks, but I was not sad. I knew this was Scott.

Lucy was a chocolate Lab we got when Scott was about 12 years old. Scott loved Lucy. She was his first hug and kiss in the morning and his last at night. During his illness, Lucy was Scott's constant companion. While he was sick, Scott gained a maturity beyond his years and was aware of his impending death. He had made his requests regarding his wake, memorial, and cremation very clear. He wanted us to donate his eyes, and then have his body cremated. His wake was to be only one day and we were to only have pictures of him present, not his ashes. He knew Lucy was getting old, so he wanted us to cremate her when her time came and put their ashes together. He then wanted us to climb up Half Dome at Yosemite, then jump off when we reached the top and spread the ashes halfway down. He was totally serious. I offered him another idea, "or we could take a walk to Half Dome, find a beautiful spot, and spread you and Lucy there." He reluctantly agreed, and two years after he died, that is exactly what we did.

Life is strange. When we least expect it, someone can be placed in front of us who can give just a bit of clarity to our inner turmoil and provide the hope we need that there is a plan and maybe even a reason. Since Scott got sick, I had struggled to make sense of why this had happened and to answer Scott when he asked, "why me?" The alternative question, "why not us", also begged an answer. But, as I talked to Diana over the course of our plane ride, the spiritual journey I had been on and continue to be on, came into clear focus. Rather than railing against fate, maybe I needed to sit back and look at what was in front of me. It had been two years since my son Scott had died from cancer and this stranger helped me see that maybe he was closer than I thought, that maybe our loved ones never really leave us.

When I got to Philadelphia, I called Gene to tell him about the plane ride. Of course, he was a little skeptical. We agreed to think about the message that Scott was sending and discuss it later.

That night when Gene and I finally got a chance to talk, I told him that I had to write the story, and he offered his support and help, including writing a few sections from his own perspective. So, here goes.

This is our story

Gene

You never know who is going to cross your path when you venture out into the universe or when you simply say hello to a stranger seated next to you on a plane. We had been spending the summer in our new South Carolina condo just outside of Charleston. Chris was to work one more year at the nursery school in New York and then we planned to sell the house the next spring and make the move permanent. But on this particular weekend, Chris was off to a farm in the country for a week with friends and horses to work with disabled kids. And I had a week as a bachelor. I dropped her off at the airport on an early Saturday morning, asking only that she let me know when she arrived at the farm. Chris is not real comfortable traveling alone and I have become much more protective of her since Scott passed. You never know when that grief will hit the surface.

At about 11:00 a.m., she called from a layover in Philadelphia. I thought she had forgotten something or, more likely, to remind me of a task to be completed before her return. No, the purpose of her call was something far more interesting and the first step in the project that brought us to these pages.

As she told you, Chris met a woman on her flight who claimed to have a connection to the other side. She could communicate with the dead. Naturally, I had always been skeptical of such people and felt that they preyed on the vulnerable, so my initial reaction was dismissive. But the more I heard, the more I became interested. The woman did not seem to want anything in return when they parted. Their interaction on the plane was the beginning and the end of their encounter. What most piqued my interest was that she did seem to have some knowledge of our son. For example, she repeated his phrase, "I got your back," which was how he promised his mom he would look over her when he was gone. She also referred to a dog. Now, I realize half the people in America have dogs, but our lab had died just a year after Scott and she said they were together. In fact, they are together, as their ashes are scattered near Mirror Lake at Yosemite. As Chris detailed their discussion, I was brought back to several incidents in the couple years since his passing in which it seemed Scott was reaching out to us, from beyond this world, trying to tell us he was okay.

After hanging up, I immediately googled this woman's name, and there she was, exactly as described. Just because one has an impressive title, though, it hardly means he or she can talk with the departed. Let's face it, our belief in this woman could be nothing more than the longing of two parents to be closer to a dear son who is no longer here. Maybe that is true, but those two women may have been brought together for a reason—a reason that is not of our understanding. Who among us cannot look back on their lives and point to a chance meeting that has changed their course, made their life richer, or simply brought some comfort? It seems that these messengers always appear at just the right time.

So, here we are writing our story. Who it reaches and what effect it will have is not for us to know. I do believe it will bring our family clarity and a better understanding of our own journey. First, we must relive a bit of our past before Scott got sick. Like most families, our lives have been a puzzle of joys, disappointments, and tears, with a good share of laughter. Our story will be told by my wife for the most part. After all, she was the one who held it together when I could not. She made the tough choices, which were always in the interest of our kids and family. Most important, she cared for a dying young man as only a mother can. I will jump in at times to offer a different perspective and possibly a bit of rebuttal.

This is our story.

PART I – Before Becoming a Couple
Chris

Before we were faced with Scott's diagnosis, our young family struggled to overcome another type of illness—addiction.

I was 21 years old, right out of college, when I first met Gene. I was still living at home, an Italian Catholic home where it was understood you did not leave unless or until you got married. Independence was never encouraged and the thought of going away to college was out of the question. Likewise, having my own apartment. Community college and marriage were to be my goals. In reality, all I ever wanted was to be a mother—that was my main goal. So I went to community college and got my Associate of Applied Science (AAS) degree in nutrition. I figured that I would work for a couple years until I got married and had children. That was just the way it was.

Gene was 28 and we were both working at a nursing home in White Plains. I was a diet tech and he was a cook. At first, we were friends. Most of the staff was young, single, and the group often would go out together after work. There was always a happy hour to go to somewhere. Gene and I had the same days off, so we would go skiing together as well. We spent a lot of time talking and getting to know each other. We had a similar sense of humor and we laughed a lot. Within six months of friendship, we began dating and enjoyed movies, restaurants, and just being together.

After about a year as a couple, we started to talk about our future. Gene was my first love and I could see myself marrying him. During this time, however, alcohol was becoming a problem in our relationship. Usually, when I went out, I was done after two drinks. Not so with Gene. Once he started drinking, he would not stop. When he drank he was never mean or abusive. He was the opposite, actually. He would get all mushy and lovey-dovey, which would really annoy me. Sometimes getting up for work the next day would be a problem for him. That would cause an argument between us, and I started to worry about him, but typically, I thought I could 'fix it'.

I was 22 years old and I really had no understanding of what alcoholism was. I thought an alcoholic lived on the streets. That was not Gene. He was kind and funny and he loved me. He was not an alcoholic in my mind. Besides, wouldn't love conquer all? We would be fine because we loved each other. Looking back, I know that I definitely believed in fairy tales, thinking we would live happily ever after. My parents did not like Gene and they kept telling me over and over how wrong he was for me. Living at home was unbearable at times because of all the friction, largely created by our relationship. Fighting with my parents only made Gene and I grow closer. It became us against them. I wanted to prove them wrong.

One night, after a little over a year of dating, Gene called me to say he was in the hospital. He said his blood pressure was very high and he really didn't know what was going on. He insisted that he didn't want any visitors. Crying hysterically, I hung up the phone. I was so worried. For three full days, I worried. Finally, Gene called. He confessed that he was really in a detox unit where he stayed those three days. He knew he had a problem and he promised to never drink again. When my parents found out, all I can remember is the two of them yelling and screaming at me, telling me over and over that he was a drunk, that he didn't love me, that all he wanted was alcohol. The way they reacted only made me shut down, pushing me away from them. I knew they were wrong, Gene did love me.

The day that Gene was discharged, his mother was having a family dinner so I went, thinking we would discuss Gene and his time in detox. I needed to understand what was really going on. We all sat around the table. His sisters Barbara and Eileen were there too, along with Aunt Grace. My face was still red from all the crying I had done. His family talked about the Yankees, football, and other mundane topics. Not one mention was made of the detox, not one. I felt like I wanted to scream; the elephant in the room was getting larger and larger. I choked down my dinner with each bite. I was afraid to bring up the subject; I felt it was Gene or his mom's place to do this. In my mind, I compared the two different family scenarios in dealing with this. On one hand was my family, yelling and screaming. On the other hand, Gene's family was passing the dinner rolls with polite conversation. It became clear that I would have to figure this out on my own. I left that night more confused than ever.

The next day, Gene and I talked. He promised not to drink again and he asked me to support him through this difficult time. He told me he loved me and I knew I loved him, so we began this journey of no drinking together. I was very supportive and pleased that we had gotten through this obstacle together which made us even closer. For the next year, Gene did not drink, but I did not understand that his disease was not being addressed, just ignored. Our relationship was getting better and we were happy. I was still working as a diet tech and Gene had begun selling cars. We got engaged and started planning our future.

My parents were not happy. In fact, the night of our engagement, they went at us for over an hour, telling us how this would never work, how we would never be able to support any children, and how this was the worst decision that we could ever make. I left the house in tears. As I was getting into the car, I looked over and saw Gene heading back toward the house. I followed him, nervous and unsure of what to expect. He walked inside and told my parents what they had just done to me was wrong. He said this was our night, and they should not have ruined it for us. If they had concerns, they should discuss them, not just scream at us about how we would never make it. I stood there amazed that he had spoken up and so proud that he did. I knew without a doubt that I was marrying this man. We set a date for April 14, 1985.

Two months before the wedding, tragedy struck. Gene stopped by his mother's house on a Sunday morning when she had not answered the phone. A birthday dinner for her at Grace's home

had been planned for later that day. When he walked in, he saw her. She was laying at the bottom of the stairs, dead. She had apparently tripped and fallen down the stairs at some time during the night. We were all devastated, especially Gene and his sisters, Barbara and Eileen. Their father had died when Gene was just 11 years old; now their mother was gone too. It was a very difficult and sad time. I wanted to cancel the wedding and just elope, but Eileen, Barbara, and Grace talked us out of it. They said their mom would have been so disappointed if we did that. She was happy for us and would have wanted the wedding to go on as planned, so we had our wedding.

Walking down that aisle, I had no doubt that this was right. After the wedding, we bought his mother's house. It was left to Gene and his sisters, so we just bought out their shares. At first, I did not want to live there. I wanted a fresh start, not the home where his mother had just died. Gene really had to convince me. The home had been in the family since 1954. It was now a two-family house, converted after his dad died. We agreed to live there for maybe, two years, and then we would buy a new home together.

For the next year Gene and I settled into married life. We worked, went out, spent time with our many friends and we truly enjoyed being together. Gene was still not drinking and we were happily planning for the next step—a baby.

Gene

The early years were good, relatively speaking. We got through my first rehab, buried my mother, and somehow got through the flack with my in-laws and managed to have some fun. As Chris said, we bought my mother's house after she died, and this proved to be our financial cornerstone and saving grace through the years. It was a two-family property and there was always some income. More important, Chris and the kids, who would be along shortly, always had a roof over their heads and equity with every payment. I often wonder what life would have been like without that house. While it carried quite bit of emotional baggage, it also provided a sense of security that I would not be able to provide—at least not then.

I was not drinking and my alcoholism was being treated by a marijuana maintenance program. It was not the most effective course of treatment, but I was giving it a try. I convinced Chris that a joint now and again couldn't hurt and she was game. Of course, my 'now and again' was more often than hers, I was nowhere near ready to take the actions of serious recovery, so my recovery was doomed to failure. But for a little while, I maintained the status quo. We were able to travel and had a solid circle of friends. Chris was working at a hospital as a diet tech and I was an adequately successful car salesman. To an outside observer, including in our own minds, life was going well.

I would like to talk about my mom for a moment. She died suddenly two months before our wedding as we were planning a birthday celebration for her on Sunday, February 3. I had been trying to get in touch with her that morning, but she was not answering the phone. I just figured she was at church or out doing something. Once it had gotten a bit past noon, I was still unable to reach her so I stopped by her house. When I arrived, her car was parked as if it hadn't moved all night. Had she already been out, the car would have been in the street because it would be used again later in the day. I sensed something was very wrong. I let myself in and found my mother's lifeless body laying at the foot of the stairs. She must have gotten up in the middle of the night, as she often did, and headed downstairs to the kitchen for a cup of coffee and fell. It was obvious that she had tumbled down the stairs hours earlier. I loved my mom as any boy or man does. Having lost my dad at 11, she was the only parent I had and to this day, I miss her very much. The most important thing I miss about her is that we could laugh together. We could look at a situation or a person, then at each other and see the humor, sometimes to the point of uncontrollable laughter. Luckily, I found this same connection with my wife. Folks who knew both my mother and my wife, say they were very much alike.

My mother's passing was a shock to all of us. We considered postponing the wedding, but since it was only two months away, that seemed impracticable. We were also pretty confident that she would not have wanted that. Right up until the last moment, we discussed foregoing the parent introductions at the reception, but they also went on as usual. In the end, I did not feel that denying Chris's folks their moment was fair. Although my in-laws were never as generous in their consideration towards me, it was not a day for recriminations. Our wedding day was a truly happy one, bittersweet as it was.

I don't want to sound like I am on a pity pot, but I have missed much in my life. I wish my dad could have been there for the father-son events. I wish my mother could have seen my children. I wish that my alcoholism had not robbed me of important events in my young family's life. Most of all, I miss my son.

Starting a Family
Chris

Our daughter, Kim, was born on December 19, 1986. She was a beautiful, healthy baby and I loved being a mom. I loved everything about it. Although looking back, like any new mom, I didn't have a clue what I was doing. I would often say that it was harder to get my driver's license. I had to study and practice to eventually pass that test, while the hospital just handed me this baby. But I loved motherhood and I loved her. I had a family now and I was so proud. It was important to me to be a good mom. As a child, I often felt alone within my own family and I was determined not to repeat the same patterns.

As much as I enjoyed my new role as mother, my marriage was getting shaky. As was inevitable, Gene began drinking again. At first he would sneak it, but then I would find the bottles. When I would confront him with the 'evidence', he would deny it and twist the situation around, so much so that I started to think I might be losing my mind. It was happening more and more.

To help with the finances, I started babysitting. I didn't want to leave Kim, so this was a perfect solution. During this time, I was Catholic. I was raised Catholic and even attended Catholic school for a while, but I didn't attend church regularly. However, on one of those rare Sundays that I did attend, I saw an advertisement in the bulletin placed by a family who needed a babysitter three days a week. The little girl, Meghan, was fourteen months. It seemed perfect—extra money and a friend for Kim. I got the job, and that was the beginning of Chris's Kids Family Day Care. I really loved caring for the girls and had a great time planning fun activities like going to the park or doing arts and crafts projects with them. Kim and Meghan played really well together, and it was a nice fit. Meghan's parents and I became good friends as well. The money I was earning was helping, especially as living with Gene was getting difficult. He was drinking a lot and there were many days when he called in sick. You can't sell cars when you're not at work! I was finding all of this scary and overwhelming.

Kim was about seven months old when I once again confronted Gene about his drinking with an ultimatum. If he wanted to keep his family, then he needed to get help. It was that simple. He agreed and soon went to rehab for 30 days. During this time, I took care of everything. I took care of Kim, our home, and also worked at the day care. I was so scared—scared of my uncertain marriage and of my family's now uncertain future.

On the weekends, Kim and I would visit Gene at the facility. He seemed very hopeful and promised he would do all he could to stay sober. Being in rehab is the easy part. The work begins when you return home. It is important for the alcoholic to attend Alcoholic Anonymous meetings several times a week to maintain sobriety. For myself, I began attending Al-Anon meetings for those whose lives are impacted by an alcoholic. This support system was vital to me and I went once a week for many years. I learned so much about myself. I had to learn how to set boundaries, how to self-love, how to think and react in a healthy way without being a caretaker, an enabler, or a people pleaser. I actually reached a point in my life where I was grateful to have married an alcoholic because it gave me personal insight I might never have had. It has been a great blessing in my life, however, after a couple of months Gene stopped attending AA meetings. He claimed he didn't feel connected to the group and insisted he could do it on his own. I tried to stay hopeful, but I was really scared.

Gene did not drink for about two years and during that time, we had our son Scott, who was born on November 29, 1988. After a somewhat difficult pregnancy and delivery, we were thrilled when he arrived. In my 24th week of pregnancy, I went into preterm labor, followed by a weeklong hospital stay, ordered bed rest and prescribed medications to halt contractions. Twelve weeks later, Scott arrived. Labor was fast and furious, totaling less than two hours. When he arrived, I noticed right away that he was blue. I remember asking the nurse about this, but she immediately gave me a shot and I soon fell asleep. The next day when I awoke, the nurse brought him to me. He wasn't blue anymore, but he did have scratches all over his face. I was told that the umbilical cord had wrapped around his neck. I think the scratches came from him trying to break free. I was so excited to hold and finally meet him. I knew he was in a big rush to get here and I promised to be a good mom to him. He clasped my finger and I fell madly in love. My life was full.

Expecting the Unexpected

Scott was a very happy baby and by the time he was five months old, he was crawling and getting into everything. I could not take my eyes off him for a minute! He was so curious and active. It would not be unusual for me to find him wrapped in the television wires or eating out of the dog bowl. By the time he was one year old he had already learned how to climb out of his crib. One morning I woke up to find him missing from his crib; he was gone! In a panic I started searching every room, convinced that he had been kidnapped. Then I heard a noise downstairs. I flew down the stairs and there was Scott, sitting on the couch and eating a cookie! When he saw me, he smiled. How did he do this? I looked around and saw that he had pushed a kitchen chair over to reach

the counter where the cookies were kept. But how did he get out of the crib? That night, after we put Kim and Scott to bed, Gene and I waited outside his door. We watched him stand up and look around. Then we saw his little leg swing over the crib, and once over, he jumped down. Happy with himself, he scooted out of the room and slid down the steps on his belly, feet first. Gene and I followed him down and caught him. Startled, he smiled. We brought him back upstairs and lowered the mattress in his crib so he could not escape.

I could not believe the mischief he could get into. I always believed someone was watching over him because sometimes his antics were downright scary. One episode really sticks out in my mind.

Scott was not yet two years old and the day care was in full swing. Kim, Scott, and Meghan were playing in the living room while I was speaking with her mom, Phyllis, in the kitchen. Meghan had been in my day care for close to four years and it was her little sister Katie's first day. As Phyllis was going over Katie's schedule, I heard a strange noise. *Screech*. We stopped talking and I heard it again. *Screech*. We walked into the living room and all I saw was Scott's head. He had removed the fireplace grate and lowered himself down the ash pit! In one quick motion I grabbed him, my heart pounding. If I hadn't come in when I did, he would have gone all the way down and probably suffocated. After that little moment of excitement, Phyllis left, and it was back to work.

Going out to stores with Scott could be quite the adventure as well. I never knew what might happen. Again, if I got distracted for even a second, he would be gone. One day while we were food shopping, I got caught up comparing prices. Of course, when I looked down, Scott had disappeared. Since this had happened before, I didn't panic. I went up and down the aisles looking for him, calling for him. As I was walking through the frozen section, something caught my eye. There was Scott, sitting in the case next to the peas, happily waving to everyone who passed. All I could do was smile, putting him back in the cart and headed to the checkout. While waiting my turn, I tried to think of any other mom who had days like these. I couldn't come up with a single person.

Kim and Scott's personalities were very different. Kim was quiet, while Scott was very outgoing. Kim thought about consequences, while Scott was very impulsive. They were both social and enjoyed the many friendships formed in the day care which was like an extended family. Since Kim was one of the oldest kids, she liked to help with the babies. Scott wanted to make everyone laugh and sometimes teased them to the point of tears. He was very active and would always find something to get into. Sometimes I would joke with my friends, saying that if Scott weren't mine, I wouldn't watch him!

Every day was an adventure for Scott and being his mom, it was for me too. I would try to predict what he might do, but sometimes I just couldn't. I learned that I just had to go with it and hope that it all turned out okay, and it usually did - then.

Parting Ways

When Scott was a toddler, Gene began struggling with drinking again. He assured me that he was not an alcoholic, that it was just the residual trauma from finding his mother dead at the bottom of the stairs. He wanted to be able to drink on weekends as lots of couples did. He said we could enjoy a few beers together on a Friday and Saturday night.

"Doesn't that sound like fun?" he said.

In my heart, I knew this wasn't right, but I wanted to believe him. I was trying really hard to cling to this marriage; there were now two children involved. Foolishly, I agreed. Within a very short time, however, Gene's weekends began on Tuesday. I knew this wasn't 'trauma drinking', it was full blown alcoholism.

By the time Scott was four and Kim was six, Gene had been to rehab two more times, always with same promise of "This time I will do it." It was exhausting. I was running the day care, taking any job I could, while Gene was bouncing from job to job. Gene would stop drinking for months at a time. There were difficult times, but there were good times as well. Life was definitely a roller coaster. We enjoyed taking the kids to the park and we had fun together, the four of us. We were working on our marriage and trying to communicate more effectively. When Kim and Scott were asleep, we would watch our favorite TV shows or a movie. We tried not to argue in front of the kids trying to present a united front. Thank God for Kim and Scott. It was because of them that I continued working hard, trying to give them the stability that they deserved. It was easier for me to focus on them than focus on myself or our problems. They had no idea that money was tight or that their dad had a drinking problem. They were young children, their days were fun and they knew they were loved. I made sure of that.

On February 19, 1993, everything changed. I will never forget that day. It was after dinner and the children were asleep. Gene came home. At this time, he was driving a taxicab, but I rarely saw any money from his job. I knew something was wrong with Gene, although I had no evidence of alcohol. I suspected he now had a gambling problem because I knew money was missing. He asked to speak with me in the upstairs bathroom. My stomach sunk with a familiar feeling. Whenever I was summoned to the bathroom, it was never good news. We sequestered ourselves inside and I sat on the hamper. He was standing in front of me, looking nervous.

"I'm addicted to crack, I don't know what to do."

"Get your stuff and get out." He was not expecting this sort of reaction. He thought I would offer rehab—again. But I was firm. Shaking with anger, I looked him straight in the eye and said, "There are two children here, and you cannot stay here with drugs. I am done. I love you, but I can't live with you. You cannot be here around my babies. Go!"

He put his things in a Hefty bag and I watched him walk away. I then called his sisters and his aunt Grace who all lived nearby. I told them what had happened and asked them not to let him in if he came by. I was adamant. Grace lived a couple blocks from us in a turn of the century Victorian home. She was born in that house and liked to say she will be taken out feet first. We had many Sunday dinners there and she loved us. Grace was someone we all turned to when things were tough and who always had a hard time saying no. Eileen also lived in town with her husband and their four children. Kim and Scott loved having their cousins, Jim, Kathryn, Mike, and Megan nearby. Gene's sister Barbara lived about 20 minutes away but it was not unlikely that Gene would reach out to her.

"Do not let him in," I repeated.

Sure enough, he showed up at their homes but they did not open the door to him. I think back now and realize what a big deal that was. They could have let him in. He was their brother and nephew, after all. I know it was hard for them, I know they cried while doing it, but they did it. Now Gene had nowhere to go. I locked all my doors and windows and I took a large frying pan to bed with me. For the first time, I was scared of Gene. He was on crack! I had seen a lot of *20/20* and was aware crack users could be violent. I knew that if he fought me, I would be ready to fight back. I checked on Kim and Scott; both were asleep. Then I went into our room and sat on the bed, crying and hugging myself and for the very first time, I prayed, I really prayed.

"Dear God, please give me strength to handle this. Please keep me strong. Please help Kim and Scott. I know that their lives are now changed forever, but I promise I will try hard to give them a good life, I promise. I'm scared, I've never been alone and now I am alone with two small children. Please help me, Amen."

I lay awake the whole night, listening for Gene. The next morning, I got up and began my regular routine. Kim and Scott got ready for school and the children arrived for day care. When the day care children left that night, I would try to explain to Kim and Scott that their dad would not be living with us anymore, it was a very long day.

That night after dinner, I sat down on the couch with Kim and Scott. They asked where their dad was, wondering if he was working late. When I told them that their dad was no longer living with us, they began to cry. I told them he was using alcohol and drugs, that was not allowed in our home. I told them how much he loved them, but he needed help to get well. I told them how much I loved them and promised that I would always take care of them. They were still crying. We cuddled together in my bed and read some books. They fell asleep in my arms, and I cried quietly while they slept.

The next day, I came up with a plan. After Kim and Scott left for school, I called their teachers and explained that their father and I had separated and asked them to please let me know how they were doing in school. While the day care children napped, I made fliers to advertise my babysitting business. At that time, Gene was unable to give me any money for child support. I was responsible for every single bill in the house and my babysitting money was just not enough. Eileen suggested stuffing envelopes for a local printing company to earn some extra money. I called to inquire about the job and received four large boxes. I don't remember how many letters were in each box, but with each one I completed, I would get $50. So, after Kim and Scott went to bed, I would sit at the dining room table and work until 1:00 a.m. I tried to do four boxes a week and did this for several months. I would get up at around 6:30 a.m. to begin work in the day care, then stuff envelopes at night. I needed this supplemental income until the day care business could build up more clientele.

Over the next several months I had no contact with Gene. Sometimes he would make a collect call to the house, but I would not accept the charges. I threw out all of his clothes, packed up everything from his closet in big Hefty bags, then I stood on the front porch and watched the trash truck haul it away. I did leave one suit hanging in the closet—a suit for his funeral. I heard that he had gone to another rehab, but once released, he chose to use again.

One June night he came by and said we needed to talk. He had decided to move to California. His Uncle John who had been sober for a long time, was there, and he offered to try and help Gene. We decided to tell Kim and Scott, all sitting together on the couch. The kids were happy to see him. I remember Scott placing Gene's hand on mine and smiling. My heart broke knowing what was coming next. Gene told them that he loved them but that he needed to move to California to get help. They began to cry. We both told them how much they were loved. I once again promised to take care of them and explained that going to California might help their dad. I remember as Gene was leaving the house, both kids ran to him, and each grabbed a leg so he couldn't leave. That was an image I will never forget. Gene left the very next day. Soon after he left, I filed for a legal separation and the following year was granted a divorce. While it was heartbreaking to see the final divorce decree, I knew it was the right thing for Kim, Scott and myself and in the long run for Gene, who had not contested this decision.

Gene leaving was actually a relief for me. It was hard, but at least I didn't have to constantly worry about him. I remained very close with his family and I am so blessed to have had such supportive and caring friends. It may seem surprising that I didn't distance myself from his family, but the reason is simple. I felt that

Kim and Scott had lost enough, I didn't want them to lose their aunts and cousins too. Besides, they loved us, and they were heartbroken and I would have missed them terribly as well. Kim and Scott were understandably sad but as their mother, I just wanted them to feel better, so six months later I planned an adventure for us. My best friend Lori and her family lived in San Francisco and she found us really cheap airfare so we could visit her. We saw all of this beautiful city and one night, we camped in Redwood Park. We were there for about four days, it was just what we needed.

Gene

Even though I was in a terrible place, I have some happy memories of those early years with the kids, especially when they were infants and toddlers. My daughter arrived first on December 19, 1986. I had never seen a more beautiful child. In the maternity ward, it was my job to get her from the nursery and wheel her tiny crib to her mother's room. Those few minutes I had alone with Kim remain so very precious to me. I can't remember now what I said to her, but I do recall the feeling that was in my heart, which I still carry with me to this very day. I don't know how addiction could be more powerful than that, but for years, it would be so for me. My son Scott came along two years later following a difficult pregnancy and an unexpectedly quick delivery of a little 'blue boy'. The cord was wrapped around his neck, but quick and excellent work by the delivery team resulted in a healthy addition to our home. Scott proved to be a handful from day one, from climbing out of his crib at one year old to taking a walk down the street at two years old, only to be corralled by a neighbor. We really were not inattentive; he just had a strong willed mind of his own and was very fast! As scared as we could be with his antics, it was impossible to resist his smile and charisma. Looking back, Scott always lived his life to the fullest as though he knew his time would be short.

What should have been the happiest time in my life turned out to be the darkest. I had a beautiful wife, two gorgeous children, but all I wanted to do was get high. I was bouncing from job to job and spending what little money I earned on drugs. By the early 90's, I had graduated from marijuana to crack and was a full blown addict. As a result, Chris had become the primary, if not sole, breadwinner. I had gotten to the sad point of being a far greater drain on the family than an asset. My desperate situation was much more evident to the people around me than it was to me. Isn't that always the case for people like me?

I was beginning to burn most of my bridges. I had been to a few more rehabs in hopes that I would somehow straighten out. I did not, and then one evening, I told Chris the true nature of my crack habit. That was the last straw, and I was shown the door. I think I slept in the woods that night.

The next couple of months were a blur. I had nowhere to go. I did another 28-day rehab program at the Veterans Hospital. When I was not hospitalized, I lived in rooming houses and drove a cab. Sadly, I had not yet hit rock bottom. After four or so months of this miserable existence, I made the decision to get out of town. My uncle John, who had been sober for decades, made me an offer to come stay with him in hopes of getting my life on track. I left for Los Angeles in June of 1993. I would not see my kids or Chris again for five years.

Moving Forward
Chris

My day care business kept me busy. I was taking care of several children, all on a part-time basis. Some children came a couple days a week, others were there several hours a day. I prayed for a full-time job. One night, I received a call asking if I would watch a little boy five days a week, 12 hours a day. When they offered the price, I put my hand over the receiver while I did a happy dance. Finally, no more stuffing envelopes! That was a turning point for the business and for our lives. I was now capable of paying all the bills, I was so happy. I would work whenever anyone needed me. If a parent had to be at work at 6:00 a.m., that was fine. I had some parents who attended night classes and would not be able to pick up their child until 9:00 p.m. Again, no problem. It was not unusual for me to feed dinner to six kids. Wanting to improve my business, I took the classes and had the home inspections that allowed me to become a licensed childcare provider. Having this license also enabled me to get on a referral list for my county. I was now getting calls from the agency asking if I had any openings. This was great because I no longer had to look for the parents, the parents were looking for me.

Kim, Scott and I settled into a stable routine. Monday through Friday, Chris's Kids Day Care was in full operation and Kim and Scott were always involved in the action. The children became like brothers and sisters, sharing in responsibilities and activities. In fact, many lifelong friendships were developed. Snack time was set aside for talking and sharing. On Saturdays, Kim and Scott enjoyed city-sponsored activities, such as swimming, baseball, or drama. I was also a Girl Scout leader for a few years. During the week, I was so busy taking care of other children that the weekends were reserved only for Kim and Scott. We loved to do hikes, bike rides and picnics together. In the winter, a great Saturday night would be having a roaring fire in our fireplace, watching a movie and snuggling on the couch. The amazing thing is that all of this was free. Even though I was able to pay my bills, I was not wasting one dime. If my girlfriends came to me to vent about their husbands or kids, I would listen and most likely offer my advice. If they spoke of divorce, they would usually say that they were most scared of doing it entirely on their own like I had to. That's true, that's me, worst case scenario!

I had also become much stronger physically and emotionally. Living with an alcoholic for years was extremely draining. I was always focused on his needs and never my own. I remember bike riding with the kids one Sunday. It felt so good, and I was having so much fun. Why didn't we ever go bike riding when we were married? Gene never wanted to, so we didn't. From then on, I swore that I would do things that made me happy. With each decision I made regarding the kids, our home or the business, my confidence was growing. I was beginning to realize that I was truly happy.

I noticed something else pretty amazing was happening. If one of my clients was leaving, for whatever reason, I found myself praying. It was always the same prayer: "Dear God, please help me find another babysitting job. Please, I'll work hard. I'll take good care of all the children. Please keep me strong, Amen."

No kidding, within a couple days, an even better job would come along, with more money and better hours. It always worked out. I used to say to Kim and Scott that my guardian angel was always watching over me. It wasn't until much later that I realized yes, maybe my guardian angel had a hand in this, but really, it was God who did the heavy lifting.

The stronger I became, the more I could do for Kim and Scott. After about two and a half years of single parenting, I had saved enough money to buy a small trailer on a campsite in the Berkshires and it was less than a two-hour drive from our home. I was working more than 60 hours a week and except for major holidays, I never took a day off. The campsite had a playground and a lake, which was perfect for us. We would leave on Friday after work and return on Sunday night. There were no phones, no television—just us. We would hike to a waterfall, ride our bikes and explore the area. At night, we would make a campfire and tell stories and eat s'mores. Sometimes their cousins or friends would come with us, but mostly, it was just the kids and me. There were many trailers on the campsite and I felt comfortable and safe there. We would go every weekend from Memorial Day to Labor Day for almost four seasons.

When Kim and Scott were 10 and 8 years old, I surprised them with a trip to Disney World. I had been planning and saving for a long time and I was so happy when it finally happened. That Easter, I put Mickey Mouse ears in their baskets. When they saw them, I told them to put on the ears, that we were leaving for Disney in seven weeks. They were so happy! We flew to Orlando that Memorial Day weekend. The Wednesday before, I closed the day care at 5:00 p.m., and we headed to the airport. We didn't get to our hotel room until after midnight. The kids quickly went to sleep and I stood on the porch outside our room, just taking it all in. We were at Disney World, I did it! We spent four magical days there. That was probably my proudest moment as a single mother.

52

Taking a Step Back
Chris

The three of us were doing well; we made a great team. I made a point to never badmouth their father in front of them. If I wanted to complain, I would call one of my friends. The kids never knew that Gene didn't send child support or that he was still struggling. It was my hope that Kim and Scott would not grow up with anger toward their father, I wanted them to know he needed help and hoped he would get it. Gene's contact with us was very limited. There were some birthdays and holidays that we wouldn't even get a call. They learned quite early not to expect anything from him, which was so sad. I tried really hard to always be there for them and to do "dad" things with Scott. I taught him how to fish, I encouraged his love of baseball, and I even watched scary movies. As he got older, Scott became very protective of me. When I would get migraines, sometimes all I could do was to get through the workday before collapsing in bed. Scott would sleep with me on those nights, just rubbing my head, and the first thing he would ask me when we woke up was if I felt okay.

My back had started to cause problems for me as well. No doubt, it was caused by the physical demands of the day care. I was always pushing a double stroller with three babies in it and my neighborhood had many hills. I usually had at least one baby on my hip, sometimes two. At first, I would be able to ease the pain with aspirin, but one day, that changed. It was the Wednesday before Thanksgiving, and when I got out of the shower, a strange sensation came over me. I can't explain it, I just felt weird. I never called in sick or took time off, but that day, I had to call my clients and explain that I wasn't feeling well. All the parents were very supportive.

I was laying on the couch as Kim and Scott were getting ready for school. Before Kim left, she brought me the phone, just in case I needed it. Soon after, I got up to use the bathroom. As I stood up, a searing pain ran down my back, all the way to my ankles. I screamed and collapsed on the floor, and no matter how much I tried, I couldn't get up. I panicked and began to cry. Then I remembered that I had the phone. I called my neighbor Gary and sister-in-law Eileen. They both came immediately. They tried to help me up, but the pain was too severe. They called an ambulance, and I was taken to the hospital. Because I didn't have insurance, the doctors only gave me an X-ray to rule out any broken bones. Eileen brought me home, and I stayed on the couch for the next four days. My friends were amazing. They helped me with dinners and my children, I was so grateful. Kim and Scott were worried about me, it was hard for them to see me in pain. Since I was stuck on the couch, they brought down their sleeping bags and spent the nights on the floor next to me. By Monday morning, I was ready for work, just trying not to push myself too hard. To prevent this type of episode from happening again, I started seeing a chiropractor a couple of times a week. However, my back was an ongoing struggle for many years and in fact was the reason for closing Chris's Kids Day Care several years later.

Although my faith was growing stronger, I no longer felt connected to the Catholic Church. While I had stopped attending Mass, I believed it was important for Kim and Scott to grow up learning about God and faith, so we all attended Sunday Mass together and they went to Sunday school for many years. When I was going through my divorce, I knew it was frowned upon in the church, so I went to a Priest for guidance on this issue. He explained that I could get an annulment, basically treating the marriage as though it never existed. I was trying really hard not to live in denial and an annulment just didn't seem right. Besides, saying my marriage didn't exist was just wrong. I never wanted Kim and Scott to feel they were conceived in anything but real love. I left that meeting feeling even more confused.

Even after this exchange, we were still attending Mass on Sundays, but it felt like we were just going through the motions. Kim and Scott had made their First Communion and continued to attend Sunday school. On more than one occasion, I would pick up Scott from class only to find his name on the board, which was not

good. The teacher informed me that Scott had been talking in class again and he wanted Scott to write 10 Hail Mary's as punishment. As we were leaving, Scott declared that he hated church. This was not what I wanted. The following week, my outlook changed again.

Shifting Gears
Chris

A tragedy we all remember, shook me to the core and became a defining moment in my life. It was the shooting at Columbine. When I heard of the incident, it felt like a kick to the stomach and I burst out crying. How could this happen? How could high school kids do this to one another? Being a mom, I thought of the killers' own mothers. How could they not know that their sons were building bombs in their bedrooms? How were they so disconnected? I knew when Scott snuck Cheez-It's into his room; I would definitely notice if he were building a bomb. I thought of the mothers who had lost their children and my heart broke for them That was it, we were making a change.

I wanted a church with an active Sunday school. I also wanted a church that offered volunteer opportunities. Basically, I wanted a church where Kim, Scott, and I felt like we belonged. I knew my parents would be upset about us leaving the Catholic Church, but I needed to do what was right for us as a family. I remember one of my former day care families telling me about their church and how much they enjoyed it. I hadn't spoken to this family in a couple years, but that afternoon, I called them. They invited us to attend their Presbyterian church the following Sunday. We went, it made such a positive impression that I remember everything about it. The sermon was titled, 'Bend or Break', meaning if you didn't bend with some traditions, they could break you. It was perfect. Scott attended their Sunday school class and enjoyed it. They taught Bible stories in a unique way, focusing on a particular story over four weeks. Each week, they learned the story in a new way. Some weeks, it was acting out the story, other weeks it was through activities like cooking or doing crafts. They also had many community outreach programs that we could get involved in together. Most important, we felt like we fit in there. For the first time, we felt like we had a church family.

As my faith was growing I could feel the support of being 'carried' by something greater, I had a literal example of it one Christmas season. Kim and Scott were in school and I had six children in my living room. I got the bright idea to go down to the basement to bring up our Christmas decorations. I planned on decorating the house when Kim and Scott got home from school, which would be fun for all the kids to do. As I headed down the stairs, I lost my footing. I remember seeing the beam in the stairs coming at my head and I screamed. The next thing I knew I was sitting on the cement floor of the basement. I looked behind me. There were about 10 steps, I had not hit any of them. There was not one bruise on my body, I never even hit that beam! I know I was carried. How else could you explain this? There were six children upstairs and it scares me to think of what could have happened if I had fallen down those stairs. I relayed the story to my friends and my kids, convinced that my guardian angel had saved me. Again, I know now that it was God.

I had been a single mother for three years when I got a phone call from Gene. Since he owed me a lot of child support, he wanted to sign over the house to me. Even though we were legally divorced, both of our names were still on the deed. I had the papers drawn up and sent to him. Just like that, the house was mine.

Gene

In 1995, I had been in California a little more than two years. I had bounced in and out of a few more rehabs. After an incident with my uncle's vehicle and a brush with the law, I found myself no longer welcome at his home and moved to a sober living facility in the San Fernando Valley, just north of Los Angeles. These are privately run residential facilities where guests pay by the week. The owners can evict you at a moment's notice and often do. This never happened to me, mainly because I was a good tenant. I met a guy named James at one of these places who helped get me a job selling printing supplies—inkjets and toner cartridges—over the phone. I figured I would do this for a while as I was getting my life together. As it turns out, I have an aptitude for this line of work and 20 years later, I still work for this company, Coast to Coast Computer Products. Little did I know that my life was about to change, finally for the better. The job did not change my life, but the positive, sober environment of that workplace made it easier to finally get sober.

About this time, I joined an AA group whose experiences were very similar to mine. I certainly was not new to meetings, but for the first time, I became part of the group rather than a cynical observer. I learned to identify, not compare. Shortly after, I moved out of sober living with James and my life seemed to finally be on track.

About a year into working on my sobriety, I had one last nightmare with cocaine. The guys I lived with asked me to leave. I moved back into a sober living house where I stayed for about three weeks. During the first few days, I could not believe I had ended up in this predicament again, I just could not stay sober. All I can remember thinking was, *I can't do this. I need help!* I dove back into meetings and did my absolute best to be honest in every situation, as well as to share openly. I don't know if I needed that last bout with drugs and the despair that went with it, but that was what it took for me. From that day to the time of this writing, I have lived a sober life. That is just one of the miracles we will share with you throughout this book.

There were many angels in my life who showed up right when I needed them. Jim and Judy, a sober couple from my group, offered me a room in their home, rather than staying in the sober living house. I was hesitant at first. Being a 40 year old man, I should have been capable of taking care of myself, but when I looked at what a mess my life was, I took them up on their offer. I was relying on someone else's judgment rather than my own.

Finally, I had a good job and a safe place to live. I was able to start sending money back to Chris in New York. It wasn't much at first, but it was consistent. Living with Jim and Judy, I always had someone to confide in, and oh, did I need them. For the first time in my life I believed I had a future that was bright. The original plan was to stay with my friends for a year, but after about six months, we made a mutual decision that it was time for me to grow up, get a place of my own, and be a productive, independent member of society. So, shortly after the New Year in 1997, I got my own place. Sober and living on my own with nobody responsible for me but me—that was huge. One day at a time, I was making it.

Chris

In May 1996, Gene got sober and wanted to start paying partial child support. He had a job and was trying to do the right thing. I appreciated that he wanted to help but did not fully trust it. Sure enough, regular child support checks began to arrive. It wasn't a lot of money, but I could tell he was trying. He also began calling the kids on a regular basis. At first, it was a little awkward, but they soon warmed up to him. The kids were happy and I was happy for them.

Gene was sober for almost two years when he asked if Kim and Scott could visit him in California. He had a consistent job and had arranged for a week off to host them. He was excited to see them and had many fun activities planned. Kim and Scott were excited too. It had been about five years since they last saw their dad. I was a little nervous, but I put on a brave face for them. So, that summer they flew to California to see him. It turned out to be a wonderful time. They went to the beach and an amusement park and met some of his friends and their kids. They were happy that their dad was back in their life. After returning home they would talk on the phone several times a week. A year later, Gene shared his plan to move back to New York; he wanted to be near the kids. He had been sober for three years by this time but I was not happy. I was thrilled he was sober, of course, but not about him moving back. I had been the one raising these kids and I felt like he was invading my territory.

Gene

My life was better than it had been in a very long time. I was sober and living a life that, a year earlier, I did not think was possible for me. I had a group of friends, my job was going well and I was making a financial contribution to my children back home. Chris was still bearing the burden of raising our kids, but at last, I was helping. A year sober turned into 18 months. I was talking regularly with my kids and they even came for a visit, giving Chris a much needed break. I took them all over town and we had a great time, but when the week was done, they were ready to return home to their mom. It was about this time when I realized I didn't want to hear about my kids' life secondhand, I wanted to be there, be part of it. I had been away from them for five-plus years, it was time to go home.

I discussed moving home to New York with Jim and Judy, as well as other trusted friends and the consensus was unanimous. Though we all agreed, I knew leaving the place I had gotten sober was going to be difficult for two reasons: First, I would be leaving my safety net, a group of people who understood, supported, and guided me. Second, and far scarier, I would be going back to the place where I had done the most damage. I would be facing my past and shortcomings head on. I had gone back the previous Christmas for a visit. My side of the family—sisters, aunts, nieces, and nephews—seemed fine, although maybe a bit nervous. They warmly welcomed me. My kids were guarded, and Chris, to her credit, was cordial—although, I am sure she was seething just below the surface. That was just a visit. What I was planning on now was permanent. I made the final decision at about two years sober, which was the summer of 1998. Then I made another trip home that Christmas to find an apartment and flew back to California to prepare for the move. This was really happening, and I had to admit, I did have fears.

When I returned, I had about five weeks to prepare, I would be driving East in February. My job graciously offered me a work-from-home position, so finding a job was not an issue. I sold what I was not taking and shipped the rest. A very big goodbye party was thrown in my honor and it seems there were a hundred people there. I was leaving many people who had become a temporary family to me. They not only taught me how to grow up, but also demanded it from me. Both in my group and at work, I had teachers who appeared just when I needed them. On February 8, 1999, I pointed my little green Nissan East and began my journey home.

Chris

Sure enough, Gene moved back. He got an apartment in Yonkers, about 20 minutes from White Plains. We tried to establish a visitation schedule, but now that the kids were a little older, 11 and 13, they had their own lives and friends. We let Kim and Scott decide if they wanted to spend the night with their dad. Some weekends, it was a yes, while others it was no. Gene had been seeing them regularly and attending their sporting events. The kids seemed fine and happy, but I was not. One day when the kids and I were driving around running errands, I asked them if they were mad at their dad for being away all those years. They both said no. I wanted to know why. It was very clear to them; he was the one who had missed out on everything. They had a good life, but he wasn't there to see it. They were happy that he was back and that he was part of their life now. I remember being stunned by their response, but they were absolutely right. It was his loss. And telling me that they had a good life—well, I'd happily take that!

That summer, I arranged a trip for us to visit Yosemite National Park, a place I always wanted to explore. Once again, we flew to Oakland, California. Lori and her three children were joining us for a road trip. One of our first stops was an old ghost town in Columbia, called Columbia State Historic Park. We had reservations at a hotel that night, so we checked into our room, left our bags, and headed out to explore. During the day there were many demonstrations and attractions, such as the blacksmith shop and the candlemaker. It was truly an old Wild West town. After dinner at the saloon, we were surprised to find that all the shops and exhibits had closed for the night. We wandered around the abandoned town, telling the kids that there were ghosts following us. They were nervously excited.

We returned to our hotel only to discover that we were locked out of the building. The "innkeepers" had left for the night! Lori and I just stood there wondering what to do. Our room was on the second floor and we could see that we had left a window open. We looked around. There was a grassy field across the road and we contemplated sleeping there, just like real cowboys. Scott had a better idea. He offered to climb up the tree next to the hotel, then swing over to the roof of the second floor and crawl through the window. No problem. Scott was the only one who could do this, so we agreed. Sure enough, he came marching down the stairs to let us in only a short time later. We clapped when we saw him.

Yosemite was beautiful, more so than I had ever imagined. We hiked, we camped, we explored. Scott loved Half Dome and said he wanted to climb it one day. It was such a fantastic trip.

Learning to Love Again
Chris

I was still having a tough time coping with Gene's move back to New York. I couldn't even be in the same room with him. Every time I tried to talk to him about what had happened, he would stop the conversation, saying he had enough guilt and that we should just move on. I wanted closure, I was very frustrated. One day we were both at Scott's baseball game. I was on one side of the bleachers, and he was on the other. I watched sadly as Kim divided her time between us. First, she sat with me for a few minutes, then she got up and sat with Gene for a few minutes. It was breaking my heart, I did not want them to be in the middle of our conflict. After the game, I called him and insisted that he hear what I had to say. He agreed and picked me up a short while later. We went to the Valhalla Dam close to my home, and the dam inside of me exploded. I began shaking, crying, and screaming at him. I might have even slapped his arm.

"How could you do this to me? You were my best friend, and you just left me and our children! How could you choose a drug over your family?"

It was quiet for what seemed like a long time. Finally, he spoke.

He never meant to hurt the kids or me. The first time he did crack, he was addicted. He knew that leaving was wrong, but he also knew that if he stayed, we would lose everything. He did all he could do at the time and hoped that I would find the strength to handle our family on my own. He apologized many times and asked me for forgiveness. As I listened, a calm came over me. I was actually grateful for the experience of being a single mom. I realized that I never knew how much strength I had. Before I knew it, I found myself forgiving him. He was not expecting this reaction and honestly, neither was I. After our talk, we went to a diner for a bite to eat. As I sat there, all red-faced from crying, I realized that I could sit across from him without any feelings of contempt. The anger was gone, and it felt wonderful. I actually felt lighter, like 100 pounds had been lifted off my back.

Now we could attend baseball games and volleyball games together. We could have discussions about the kids and come to a resolution together. Soon, we even began laughing together. After about six months, I realized something. I was falling in love with Gene again, which was a little scary. Truthfully, it was very scary. What if he hurt us again? He was sober now, but what if he used again? Could I ever fully trust him again? I didn't have the answers to any of these questions. Then, one day, Gene told me he still loved me. We agreed to try dating, but we didn't tell anyone, especially Kim and Scott. It was top secret. That way, if it didn't work out, Kim and Scott wouldn't be disappointed. So we were a secret couple.

We would usually meet at a restaurant somewhere outside of White Plains and spend time getting to know each other again. We had both changed since the last time we dated. Back then, I was young, still living at home, believing in the fairy tale. Now, I was mature and confident, able to handle almost anything. Gene was still funny and kind, I could see that he was becoming more mature. On top of that, now he was sober. We were both better versions of ourselves. After about six months of our clandestine relationship, we knew that we wanted to get married again but didn't know how to tell our kids, our family or our friends.

I called my pastor and asked him for guidance. He recommended a family counselor. So, the four of us attended family counseling for approximately six months. Some issues concerned the kids, so they would join us at those sessions. Other issues pertained to only Gene and me, so we would go without the kids. We were working very hard at repairing our family.

Gene started attending church with us on Sunday mornings. It was important to me and I wanted him to be as involved with us as a family. Our minister, Don, asked us to be youth leaders for the church. We held this position for five years, which only brought us closer.

Initially, we were going to remarry on our original wedding day, April 14. After realizing that the *Titanic* sank, Lincoln got shot on that day, and our first marriage was so troubled, we decided on a new date. One of my day care clients had a condo in Vermont and offered it to us for Columbus Day weekend. I remember calling our minister the Tuesday before and telling him that we wanted to remarry. I asked if he could perform the ceremony that week. He said Thursday would be fine and his wife, Donna, along with his associate pastor, could be our two witnesses. So instead of waiting until April, Gene and I eloped with the kids on Thursday, October 12, 2000.

We were married in the chapel at our church. Don, our minister, gave a beautiful talk about second chances, and after the ceremony, we all went to dinner to celebrate. Later that night, we went to Eileen's home to tell her and the kids the news. We then called Barbara and Grace to tell them as well. They were all happy for us. Now I had to tell my parents—not an easy call to make. Nervously, I dialed. My mother answered. I simply told her that Gene and I had gotten married again. First, there was silence, then she offered her congratulations, as did my father. After I hung up, I felt relieved. We were married again, we were a family again. The next morning, we drove to Vermont, the four of us on a honeymoon. We were so happy.

Gene

After a long, cross country drive, I arrived in NY to a cold February rain, a sharp contrast to the perfect Southern California weather. There were many emotions in those early days being back home. I was thrilled to be back with the kids but also knew that there were more than a few folks who were less willing to greet me with open arms. First among that group would be Chris, then her family. The kids at first were guarded but warmed quickly. My sisters, nieces and nephews, the same. That guy who had left nearly six years earlier was a train wreck, so any caution was more than understandable. I had been home the previous two Christmas holidays, but now this was the real deal.

I settled into my apartment about 20 minutes from Chris and the kids. Very gradually I began to integrate into Kim and Scott's lives by attending their games and school events while they would occasionally spend the night at my place. Chris and I very early on had little interaction, save the icy glances. My being back in New York had altered the status quo. This all came to a head at one of Scott's little league games. Chris and I were sitting in different bleachers as Kim ran back and forth to spend time with us both while Scott was on the field. The next day to her credit, Chris called me and suggested we get together to clear the air as we could not go on this way. By this time it was June and on a beautiful evening we went for a ride, just the two of us. We stopped at a park to talk and she just ripped into me, letting forth with a heart full of justifiable anger. Several times I wanted to rebut but knew she was right, so I kept quiet. I had it coming, she deserved this moment. The aftermath was remarkable. While I am sure she was emotionally drained, her entire demeanor was different. Her eyes had softened and the edge in her voice was gone. We were far from any sort of reconciliation, but co-existing now seemed possible. In hindsight, that day was a turning point towards a brighter future as a family.

Summer eventually turned into Fall, the kids were back in school and my role in the family was increasing. I was attending Kim's volleyball games, taking part in parent teacher nights and doing many of the things that I had missed for so long. Chris and I were getting along and began spending time together. At first it was just in relation to the kids, but before too long it was because we were beginning to enjoy each other's company again. We began to see the good in each other which, until recently, had been buried below a mountain of troubles. As had happened when we first met, a friendship again developed which quickly developed into romance. It was both exciting and frightening and possibly against our mutual good judgement, but some things are just meant to be.

Our kids were happy to have two parents again. There was no doubt of a new dynamic for all. What up until recently was three, was now four. There were rough spots, new boundaries needed to be set all the time respecting what had been. The life before dad could not and would not be forgotten, but the road forward included all of us and I can honestly say, through hard work, that we all did well. On October 12th 2000, Chris and I were remarried. Kim was the Maid of Honor and Scott my Best Man. We had come full circle for the better and we would need every ounce of strength a family could muster.

Returning to Normal
Chris

Soon, everyone settled into a normal routine. Gene wanted to be the one getting the kids up for school and I welcomed it. I was able to sleep an extra half hour before beginning the day care since Gene would now be handling the morning routine. Now, I was real strict concerning sick days. In order for Kim or Scott to stay home, they had to have a high fever, vomiting, or a doctor's note - preferably all three. One morning, I heard Kim come down the stairs.

"Dad, I don't feel well," she said.

I was awake, ready and waiting to hear his answer, wondering if I would have to intervene. There was silence. Finally, Gene spoke.

"Kim, you know I don't have that kind of authority, go ask Mom," he said, pointing to our bedroom.

I was giggling with delight at his response, Kim resigning herself to go to school.

Around this time, we made part of our bedroom an office for Gene. He worked in our bedroom while I worked in the living room with the children. All the children loved him and he would venture out every so often to see them. About two weeks after we got married, we adopted Lucy, a beautiful chocolate Labrador retriever. Life was good. Gene and I were happy, so were Kim and Scott. Our lives were very busy with work, school, sports, and church. Gene was attending AA meetings regularly and I was supportive and grateful.

Then, a year after our remarriage, we were faced with yet another tragedy on September 11. I was in the living room with the children after having finished breakfast. Gene called me into the bedroom where the television was showing footage of the planes crashing into the Twin Towers. We were both in shock, this was happening only about 30 miles from our home. I went back into the living room and began to read the children a book, but my nerves continued to grow. Gene came into the living room and motioned for me to go into the kitchen. He then told me about the next two plane crashes. We were both scared. The only thing I knew for sure was that I wanted Kim and Scott at home with me.

We came up with a plan. I called the day care parents and suggested that they pick up their children. Every parent agreed and quickly arrived. Then Gene and I went to the middle school and high school to pick up Kim and Scott. I didn't know what would happen, but at least we were all together. That afternoon, we were glued to the television set, still in shock and disbelief. The church had contacted us about holding a service that night and it was Scott who suggested we all attend. I am so glad we did. It was a wonderful service and we felt such a connection. During this time, people were seriously questioning God. "How could God let this happen?" or "This proves that there is no God." I remember thinking that God was crying with us. He hadn't caused this to happen, it saddened him. I also knew that believing in God and having faith was the only way to get through this.

On November 15, 2001, I would celebrate my 40th birthday. So many people give so much thought to their birthdays, but honestly, I am not one of those people. Gene really wanted me to have a party and promised to do all of the work. It took a while to convince me. Although I am pretty outgoing; I do not like to be the center of attention. When the day arrived, however, I must admit, I was very excited. That afternoon, my friend Amy took me for my first manicure and pedicure. All my life, I would pass by those nail salons and now I finally had the chance to be pampered. It was wonderful and I am happy to say, is something I have continued to do. That evening, our home was filled with family, friends and lots of amazing food. As I was giving my 'speech,' I mentioned how grateful I was for my wonderful children, my family and friends. I also said how blessed I was that Gene and I were together again. That night as I lay down, I thought what a lucky duck I was. I had a great life.

Gene

Resuming life as a family was even better than I had hoped. Chris and I were doing well and the kids were becoming more involved with their friends and lives beyond our home. As is often the case, my big worry of remarriage was that the past would be a constant issue, especially during conflicts, but happily that was not a problem. Although our history certainly was not swept under the rug, it was never used as a weapon. We got a dog, we went to church as a family, and Chris and I worried about our kids. Not long after, along with every other American, we experienced September 11th. It was a shock, we talked, we grieved for the fallen and held our children a bit closer. We were grateful it did not directly touch our family, it just happened so close to home.

Growing Pains
Chris

During elementary school, Scott was diagnosed with
learning disabilities which we believed to be the result of a
momentary lack of oxygen at birth. He had been receiving speech
therapy since age three. He repeated kindergarten and was placed
in multisensory classes. Children handle learning disabilities in
many different ways. Scott's way was to become the class clown, a
natural outgrowth of his outgoing personality and sense of humor.
He was very quick witted and always looking for a laugh. He was
also a prankster. One prank really stands out in my memory. He
was in fifth grade. As everyone was leaving school that day, he
turned to a classmate, Jeremy, and said that he couldn't believe
they had an entire book report due tomorrow, some book they were
reading in class. Then Scott quickly boarded his bus as Jeremy
went home in a panic. He told his mom that he needed to go back
to school to get this book because he had a big report due. His
mother drove him to school, but it was closed. They went
searching for another copy of the book and found it at a library.
They called other classmates but no one knew about this big book
report. "Scott McMurray says it's due tomorrow," the child said.
Soon, several sets of parents and children were working through
the night to finish the book report. The next day, five very weary
children handed in their reports. The teacher stared at them
blankly. There was no book report due. Scott had made up the
whole thing! That morning, the principal called to inform me that
Scott would receive detention for this and asked what punishment I
would be giving at home. I told the principal that I wouldn't be

punishing him. My three-year-old's in the day care knew how to question something. Why would his classmates and parents listen to what Scott McMurray had to say? Scott was 10 years old at the time. I am still amazed at this prank, I still think it's funny.

Scott still struggled with school. He was very social and popular—and very mischievous. We received many phone calls from the administration regarding his latest antics. Scott's fourth grade teacher summed it up perfectly when he said, "I wish that I were Scott's friend because he is so much fun, it's just so hard being his teacher."

Having fun, making others laugh, that was Scott's priority. Schoolwork—not so much.

By the time Scott reached middle school, his learning disabilities were becoming more problematic. In elementary school, he was in one classroom and the teachers helped with organization, which was especially difficult for him. In middle school, however, he was changing classes up to nine times a day and he was having trouble keeping track of all his assignments. At the beginning of each year, I would give him different color notebooks for each subject and I was constantly reminding him to write in his planner. Despite these efforts, Scott still struggled. We had him evaluated by the educational psychologist and were saddened to discover that he was actually two grades behind in reading and math. The tests also showed poor fine motor skills and short-term memory problems. We put tutors in place and he was receiving services provided by the school. He would have extra time on tests and would type out his assignments instead of writing them. There were many conversations with the teachers and Gene and I could get very frustrated with Scott, who struggled to take school seriously.

Scott would never accept the learning problems and would never ask for help. He continued to cope by acting out as the class clown. Disrupting the class was easier than being called on and not knowing the answer. Scott never failed a class, and he never had to go to summer school. He always managed to get by, but Gene and I took note of one variation. If Scott had a younger male teacher, he was excited and engaged in that class, but it was often a struggle with an older female teacher, whom he would consider 'boring'. If you asked Scott, he would tell you that he liked middle school. He had many friends and he certainly had a good time. He clearly had a better time than most of his teachers did!

By the end of eighth grade, we had decided to have his educational level tested privately. We hoped to find a professional who could help guide us to a high school that would benefit Scott. The local school was so large that we worried he wouldn't find success there and the school in White Plains that specialized in learning disabilities did not have a high school. After many hours of testing, the director called us in to discuss the results. She confirmed that he had a language-based disability and that he was still approximately two grades behind in reading and math. I asked her what she would do if this were her son. She felt that a high school specializing in learning disabilities was his best option. Because there were none locally, our only choice was sending him to a boarding school. My heart sank, I didn't want this, I wanted him home with us. She went on to explain that children with learning disabilities who do not receive proper guidance, face a very uncertain future, often beginning with cutting classes, then self-medicating with drugs and alcohol and finally dropping out of school and running away from home. I was crushed. I remember crying the entire ride home.

The next morning, Gene and I spoke with Scott. We told him what the specialist had recommended. He started to cry; he didn't want to go to a boarding school. He wanted to go to the local high school with all his friends. We explained that we wanted him home with us, but we were afraid that the local school could not help him succeed. We knew that he was very smart; he just needed to learn the tools in order to achieve. He promised that he would do everything to help himself. We agreed to keep him at home, but we had to see that he was doing his part. He was required to attend every class, as well as his tutoring sessions. He also had to play a sport or join a club each semester. Outside of school, he would complete his confirmation classes and participate in the church youth group. If he didn't follow this plan, then he would have to go to a boarding school the following year. That was the deal. He agreed to it and we even signed a contract. We were all very hopeful.

Scott graduated from eighth grade and enjoyed a wonderful summer. He worked as a camp counselor for the nursery school associated with our church and spent time with family and friends. He was excited about starting high school in September. As a freshman, he joined the football team and took a part in the school play. In addition to his other church activities, he had a private tutoring session every Monday night. He was averaging a C in his classes and seemed to be keeping up his end of the bargain, or so we thought.

Toward the end of the school year, I received a phone call from the attendance office. Scott had just been caught cutting class and as she looked up his records, she noted that his attendance seemed "spotty". I asked for more details. Apparently, Scott had cut 27 classes in the course of the year. I was furious! It was the end of May and they were just noticing this behavior? This had been my fear all along, that there were too many kids in this school and Scott could slip between the cracks. I spoke with Gene, I was pretty hysterical. I was so pissed because now I would have to follow through on the contract. I didn't want Scott to go to boarding school, but I felt that I had no choice. The specialist said it would start with cutting classes, and he was right! The second step could be self-medication and I was not going to let that happen. I did some research and found a school in Florida that specialized in learning disabilities. They had an opening in September for Scott's sophomore year, so I made an appointment for the three of us to visit the following week.

When Scott got home that afternoon, Gene and I had a talk with him. We told him about the phone call from the school office. Although there had been many positive behaviors that year, we were afraid for him academically. He was so smart and creative, but he would not succeed at that high school. We reminded him of the contract and informed him that we would be visiting a school in Florida. He was upset and refused to go, but Gene and I were not giving in this time. If we did, his sophomore year would only be worse. My heart was breaking because I truly didn't want Scott to go, but I knew it was something we had to do.

The next week we visited the school. By the end of the tour, Scott agreed to go. I was not looking forward to August, I was going to miss both of my babies. Scott would be leaving for school in Florida at the end of the month and Kim would be leaving at the same time for college.

The summer before boarding school, Scott continued to work at the church camp and hung out with his friends. He was not excited about the new school, but he knew he had to go. I was not happy about it either, but I tried to be positive for him. About a week before we were supposed to leave for Florida, a hurricane hit. Parts of the school were damaged, so the start of classes were delayed. A month later, we brought him to Florida and just before moving him into his dorm, another hurricane hit! I remember thinking that maybe this was a sign and we should bring him home to White Plains. I even called the high school and explained the situation, but school had been in session for about a month now and Scott would be very far behind. The boarding school was delayed for a few more days and then we could finally bring him to campus. We then learned that the administration had decided to house the students and some staff at a hotel for a few weeks while parts of the school were being reconstructed. That meant I couldn't even set up his room and I had to say goodbye in the parking lot. I began to cry - I mean hysterical, ugly crying. I couldn't say goodbye, I didn't want him to stay. I was a real mess, so much so that the principal had to put me in the car. I watched as Scott walked away with the other kids and I was still sobbing as Gene drove us to the airport. Scott called to tell me that he was fine and he asked me to please stop crying. I slowly tried to get it together.

For the first few months, Scott seemed to be doing well. He was making friends and enjoying some of his classes. When he came home for Christmas, he told us that he wanted to come home for good. I said we would discuss it at the end of the year, when school was over. After the holidays, Scott returned to boarding school—not happy, but resigned to it. His grades were averaging a C, but he did not have much motivation. I was hoping his study habits would improve, but honestly, I was not seeing much of a difference between the two schools. That is when it clicked for me; Scott had to be the one who wanted it. Since Scott wanted to come home to school, I wondered how he would do. I was hoping he would get all A's and promise to keep it up for the rest of his academic life. Wouldn't that be nice?

In April, we got an unexpected phone call from Scott. He had been expelled. He was caught coming in from the woods with a group of kids where there was pot smoking. We were devastated. Gene made plans to fly to Florida the next day. When they arrived home, Scott looked shell-shocked. He was very remorseful. It was definitely a low point in all of our lives. We got another surprise when we called the school to get the results of his drug test. It was negative! He had admitted to smoking, so how could it be negative? To this day, I don't really know. Did he admit to it because he wanted to come home? I know he was with this group of kids, their tests came back positive, but somehow Scott's did not. Because of the test results, the administrator said Scott could return to school, but we said no. How could they expel him before knowing the results? I felt uncomfortable with this school now. I was assured that a drug expulsion would not appear on his permanent record, but rather, it would reflect that he had voluntarily left the school. A couple of days later, he was back at the local high school and picked up where he left off with the many friends he had left behind. This was one of Scott's greatest strengths and helped him to navigate the difficult experience of the Florida boarding school. Scott's social skills and caring nature helped him to make good friends easily. In his short time in Florida he made lasting friends and in fact, one of his last 'road trips' was made with a friend he made during this time and stayed with him until the end.

Challenging Authority

About a month after his return, Scott brought home a permission slip for a class trip to Great Adventure, an amusement park in New Jersey, which is more than a two hour drive. The trip was a special activity for his chemistry class, they were going to measure the speed and distances of the roller coasters and other rides (this is not chemistry – it's physics!!). The note also said that due to being such short notice, the cost for each student would be $90 cash, no checks. The bus would leave school grounds the Friday of Memorial Day weekend at 8:00 a.m. sharp and return by 7:00 p.m. I thought this sounded like a great trip and signed the permission slip. The next morning, I gave Scott the $90.

Later, Gene voiced his concerns. He was suspicious of the trip. He didn't believe that a class trip would travel all the way to New Jersey, especially the Friday before a holiday weekend. I thought Gene was paranoid and I told him as much. We saw the permission slip, it was printed on the school stationery. Scott couldn't have made up such a trip. The tension between us continued to mount. Why would he doubt a class trip? Besides, with all that we had just gone through with the boarding school, Scott wouldn't betray us and blatantly deceive us.

"No, I told Gene, you are wrong."

The night before the trip, Scott and I were at the mall buying him clothes for his summer job at the country club. He was a camp counselor, so he needed shorts and collared shirts. As we got into the elevator, Scott asked me why his dad would doubt the trip. I couldn't give him an explanation because I didn't know the answer. He then asked me why I believed him. I expressed my faith in him. After all we had been through, I didn't think he would lie to us. He nodded, and we went home.

The next morning, Scott left for the trip. A few hours later, Gene called.

"Sit down, I have to tell you something. There is no class trip. I just called the school, they had no idea what I was talking about."

It felt like a kick to my gut, my whole body shook with fury. I called the school myself, there had to be an explanation. The administrators confirmed that there was no class trip to Great Adventure. I hung up the phone, feeling more betrayed than ever. I had believed in him and stuck up for him. I called around to figure out which group he had gone with on the trip. I wasn't just angry, I was scared. These kids only had a junior driver's license, so they were inexperienced with this kind of driving. They would have to cross bridges and take major highways to get there. I actually got the phone number of one of the kids, so I called and asked to speak with Scott. When he got on the phone, I shared my knowledge of the scam and demanded that he come home immediately. I then spoke with the other kids' parents, alerting them to the reality of the situation, but all of them refused to believe me.

A few hours later, Scott came home. I approached him the moment he walked through the front door. I yelled at him for betraying me, then slapped him across the face. Twice. Looking back, this is something I wish I hadn't done. In fact, it has become one of my biggest regrets. At the time, I didn't see any other way to get through to him. I didn't think grounding him would do any good, and I never could have predicted that, a couple of years later, he would get sick and die. So, I live with this regret. Because Gene

and I notified the school, Scott would have to serve detention for
cutting class. He was the only child to receive any punishment.
Although there were probably 10 kids in the group, no other parent
acknowledged their child's involvement.

Do you want to know how Scott concocted this whole
plan? He went to his study hall teacher and told her that he needed
help with his so called 'English project'. He told her the
'assignment' was to create a permission slip. The study hall
teacher actually gave him the school letterhead and helped him
with the wording. No wonder it looked so professional! For many
years, this was a sore subject for me. Whenever it was brought up,
I would just get furious all over again. As the years went on, Scott
would occasionally remind me of the incident and wondered why I
still got mad. During Scott's final weeks, we were sitting in his
room, listening to music. Again, he asked me why it still bothered
me. He had hurt me by lying. Despite my ongoing support, he had
betrayed me. He had never thought of it that way, and he was truly
sorry. That day, he must have apologized ten times. I was just
happy that he finally understood. Looking back, now that he is
gone, I must admit the stunt was so clever. No one else could have
pulled that off but Scott.

Scott's junior and senior years of high school were good
but fairly typical. Kim had graduated from high school in 2004 and
was studying Political Science and Peace and Justice issues at
Villanova University. Scott had an active social life, played
varsity baseball, got his driver's license and had many friends.
Social skills were one of Scott's greatest strengths and he was as
good a friend to others as they were to him. He experienced his
first love, and as a mother, it was wonderful to see him treat a girl

with kindness and respect. I was proud of him. He was also involved with the Jiggy Showcase, a rather offbeat talent show at school.

During the Summer of 2006, I was preparing to close Chris's Kids Family Day Care. My back issues finally caught up with me and it became necessary to undergo spinal fusion surgery. Because of the extended recuperation time, all of my families would need to make other child care plans and we decided that it was now time to end that phase of our lives. That decision, however, was not made without serious trepidation. It was not the surgery or the recuperation that scared me; I was worried about my life after Chris's Kids. It had been a part of my life for so long that it had become part of my identity. What would I do? What could I do? What did I even want to do? I soon found out that God had other plans for me.

Scott challenged us during those years as well. He would break curfew or question our authority. As parents, we tried to be fair, but I'm sure he didn't see it that way. One day, I was in the kitchen when I overheard Kim and Scott talking in the living room.

"Mom's not our friend," Scott said.

Well, you're not my friend either.

"Yeah, she's Mom," they finally agreed.

That's right. I'm not your friend, I'm your mom.

After his return from Florida, Scott approached his studies with a bit more diligence although still struggling in some areas. With extra help, tutoring, and a bit of increased awareness, he graduated from high school and looked forward to attending college in the Fall of 2007.

Scott's high school graduation was a great night. He looked so handsome, we were so proud.

That summer, he worked and hung out with his friends, and before we knew it, it was time to get him ready for college. It was an exciting day when we arrived at his school. We set up his dorm room, bought him his books, and walked around campus. Gene and I hugged him goodbye and hoped for the best. We never would have thought that, in a few months, our lives would change forever.

Gene

I was working in an office off our bedroom and the rest of our house was dedicated to Chris' Kids Family Daycare. It got a bit loud at times but it was working. But as those early years of remarriage rolled by, it became evident that the years of watching children had taken its toll on Chris' back. So much so that it was determined she would eventually need surgery, which also meant she would close her business. This would, of course, mean that I would become the sole breadwinner, a scary prospect. Like everything else in my life of sobriety, I faced it one day at a time. Since surgery was scheduled for the middle of September, Chris' Kids Family Day Care officially closed at the end of August 2006.

Simply put, Chris' business was an amazing enterprise that touched so many lives in many positive ways and paid the bills. It was a big part of our story. On a daily basis our home was filled with anywhere from two or three to ten or more children, mostly not our own. There were toys, snacks and ongoing 'ring around the rosy'. There was naptime, story time, and quite a few time outs. Chris did it all. When it did all finally come to an end, there had to be some kind of tribute, a day to recognize what it all meant. Kim, Scott and I planned a party and invited as many of the families and kids we could contact. That's quite a few over a twenty- year period. We surprised Chris with a gathering of kids and parents, all who had mostly wonderful memories of their time in our home. It was a great day. To this day, ten plus years since she closed shop, Chris will receive a phone call or a note from one of her 'kids' with a remembrance or just to say hello. Don't get me wrong, the money was needed and that was what set the daycare in motion, but the legacy will forever be the relationships among Chris, Kim, Scott and the kids who came and were a part of it every day.

Now the business was closed and I was fully responsible for the family financially. Chris had a lengthy surgery to repair her back and faced a difficult recovery. I, with the help of my boss, rented some office space and hired a couple of guys and was building up my commission only sales force. There was trepidation for all involved, myself included, that this all new dynamic was going to work. Day by day, bill by bill, it was getting done. As a family we had come full circle.

PART II - During
December 31, 2007
Chris

I was very excited and hoped that the New Year, 2008, would be a great year. So many good things were happening with our family.

Gene and I were doing great as a couple; our marriage seemed stronger than ever. At this time, we had been remarried seven years after an eight year divorce. I had closed my twenty year, home day care business in 2006 due to spinal fusion surgery. The recovery took about six months and I was finally pain free. Kim, age 21, and Scott, age 19, were both home from college for Christmas break. Kim was a senior at Villanova University and had recently been accepted to their master's program, which would begin right after her graduation in May. Since she was a little girl, Kim always knew that she wanted to make a difference in this world and now with an undergraduate and soon a graduate degree in Political Science and Peace and Justice, she was on her way. We were excited and proud of her. Scott had just completed his first semester at the State University of New York at Delhi.

We were thrilled when he was accepted to Delhi. I didn't have high expectations that he would suddenly turn into a great student. I was happy that he was moving out for a few months!

So, here we were on New Year's Eve. Both kids had made plans with their friends. Scott was sleeping at a friend's house because there was a party in that neighborhood and I was just glad that no one would be driving. We ate pizza together and then everyone got ready for the night. Before he went out, Scott complained of a pain in his neck. I asked him if he wanted to stay home.

"It's New Year's Eve, of course I'm going out!" he said.

I gave him two aspirin and told him to have a good time. I figured it couldn't hurt that much if he was still going to the party. Gene and I, along with his sister Eileen, went to see the movie *Juno*. As we ate popcorn and laughed, we never would have guessed that our lives were about to change forever. That was to be our last 'normal' night. Happy New Year 2008.

January 1, 2008

I was awakened by a phone call around 6:30 a.m. It was Scott.

"Mom, can you pick me up? I don't feel good."

I dressed quickly and told Gene about the situation, then left immediately to go get Scott. He was waiting for me outside. When he got in the car, I noticed he looked pale. His neck was stiff and he appeared to be in pain. Scott had been pledging a fraternity, so I thought he might have pulled a muscle. Thinking he would refuse, I offered to take him to the emergency room. He agreed without hesitation. Now I knew something was really wrong.

As soon as we got to the emergency room, I explained that he was 19, living at school and complaining of a stiff neck. Immediately, they isolated him, thinking it could be meningitis. I wasn't worried about this because he'd had the vaccination right before the semester began. Scott was insistent about the sharp pain in his neck so the doctors decided to do an MRI. The results showed "trauma" to his neck. They asked him if he had been in an accident. The answer was no. They continued with more questions, asking if he had felt light headed. Scott mentioned that he had passed out a couple of weeks before. This was news to me. The doctors then ordered a chest X-ray. When the results came back, they said his lungs were filled with nodules, which could be a type of pneumonia. At this point, Gene and Kim arrived at the hospital. We were all just hanging out with Scott, trying not to worry. The doctors wanted to admit Scott so they could run a few more tests. They were going to call a doctor from infectious disease. "We will have more answers tomorrow," they said. We got Scott settled in his room and left around 9:00 p.m., telling him we'd be back first thing in the morning.

When I returned to the hospital at 9:00 a.m., a doctor was already with Scott. During the night, they had performed a CAT scan and discovered a mass in one of his kidneys, so they were scheduling more tests. Getting nervous, I called Gene and he arrived immediately. We were all trying to stay positive. The doctors said it could be pneumonia, lung disease, or a malignancy. They were ordering a bone marrow test and a PET scan. We stayed with Scott the entire day, then left again at 9:00 p.m. I kissed him goodbye and told him I'd be back in the morning. When we got home, we explained the situation to Kim. We refused to believe it was a malignancy. It was probably pneumonia. we'd even take a lung disease, just not a malignancy.

When I returned to the hospital the next morning, I saw Scott's face was red from crying. He was alone.

"Scott, what's wrong?" I asked, entering the room. Scott turned to face me.

"They said I have cancer, Mom!" he cried. "Where is your God now? Where is your God?"

I was taken aback by this question. I had a split second to answer, and I knew this was an important moment. I had to choose my words carefully because the way I responded could crush Scott's faith and that I wouldn't do. So, I walked over to him, hugged him tightly, and said, "He's right next to you, bud, he's right next to you." Then we both sobbed.

Until pathology arrived with the diagnosis, we didn't know what type of cancer Scott had. All we knew was that it was very aggressive. His lungs, lymph nodes, kidneys, blood, and skeletal system were all affected. One doctor said we should hope for advanced lymphoma, because this cancer is treatable with a very high cure rate.

We asked for Scott to be released, we just wanted him home. By now, our family, church, and friends knew what was happening. Some people called, others stopped by. We were appreciative of all their concern. Whatever this was, I knew we weren't alone. As Scott lay on the couch, he began to shiver. Noticing this, I put a blanket over him, and I asked him why he didn't ask me for one. He said he didn't want to bother me.

"Taking care of you is an honor, whatever you need, please tell me."

That night, he said his back was sore and he wanted to sleep in bed with me. He was 19 years old and hadn't slept in my bed since he was a little boy, but we both needed comfort, so I moved over and he climbed in next to me. I began to rub his back. As I did, I prayed.

"Dear God, please, when I wake up, please let it be me who is sick, not my son, not Scott. Please let it be me."

We soon fell asleep. When I awakened, at first I was disoriented, then I looked next to me and saw Scott. Then I remembered. Tears filled my eyes.

It's not me.

A few days later, White Plains Hospital called to schedule an appointment with an oncologist to discuss Scott's test results. We all went to the appointment. Kim took the notes because she was calmer than Gene and me. The doctor was still waiting on pathology, but it was apparent that this was a very aggressive cancer. She had ruled out advanced lymphoma, but a possible cause was Ewing's sarcoma. She recommended a hospital in New York City where this type of cancer had been treated before, she also felt that a children's hospital would be better for him.

"Am I dying?" Scott asked.

The doctor responded that only a few people had survived treatment for Ewing's sarcoma.

That's all I remember. I left the room in a daze and wandered down the hallway. I found a corner and collapsed in tears. A few minutes later, Gene, Kim, and Scott found me there. Gene helped me up, and we made our way to the car. Gene and Scott sat in the front, Kim and I were in the back, away from Scott's view.

"That was fun," Scott said sarcastically.

I gripped Kim's hand and screamed without making a sound. I didn't want Scott to see me. I was writhing in the backseat, continuing to squeeze Kim's hand. When we got home, Scott went to his room, I collapsed again on the dining room floor.

"Not my son! Not my son!" I screamed.

After a couple of minutes, I knew I had to get it together. I went to Scott's room. He was laying in bed, listening to music. I sat beside him, my face red from crying.

"I love you," I said. "I will help you with whatever you need, I promise."

He just nodded.

By this time, so many people had called. Because Scott was such a practical joker, some of his friends didn't know if what he was telling them was true, so many of his friends' parents called to confirm and offer their support. I had to tell them it was true. Scott did have cancer, we just didn't know what kind.

Our good friend from church, Beverly, is also a doctor at Montefiore Medical Center in the Bronx. She informed us that a team of doctors had come from Memorial Sloan Kettering Cancer Center (MSKCC) to run the Pediatric Oncology Service at The Children's Hospital at Montefiore (CHAM). She had already spoken with the chief oncologist, Dr. Richard Gorelick, and he was expecting our call. We contacted him immediately and arranged to meet the next day. When we arrived, we met a wonderful team of doctors who always respected Scott's wishes – even when they might not agree – who were incredibly supportive of him until the very end. We were still waiting on pathology, but Scott was admitted for a procedure to insert a Broviac line in his chest. It would have three extensions for chemotherapy and other medications. This way, as soon as pathology came back, he could begin treatment.

A few days later, we learned Scott's diagnosis, which was called desmoplastic small round cell tumor (DSRCT). It is a very rare pediatric cancer that affects approximately twenty children a year in the United States, with approximately 200 cases worldwide and it is most common in boys, ages 14–22. The doctors explained that this cancer is DNA based. A molecule from one strand of DNA hops to another strand and once it starts, it spreads very quickly. Scott's prognosis was poor, in fact we were told a two-year survival was optimistic. We knew the treatment would be brutal, but we were praying for those two years. However, the odds were that he would die. As if one scenario was better than the other?

After hearing this, I began thinking about Scott's life. Subconsciously, Scott must have known that he would die young.

From the time he was a toddler, he lived every day to the fullest. Scott was very impulsive and spontaneous, rarely giving thought to the consequences. He would say, "*Present* Scott cannot worry about what trouble *future* Scott gets into." Who thinks like that?

I remember a time when Scott was about eight years old. After school was snack time and all the day care children, plus Kim and Scott, would sit together at the kitchen table. As they were eating, I would start a conversation. On this day, I asked each child to think about what they wanted to be when they grew up and why. I then went around the table to each child. Their responses consisted of a fireman, a policeman, an actress, even a marine biologist.

When it became Scott's turn, he looked at me very seriously and said, "I can't picture myself growing up, I can't picture myself being an adult."

I told Scott I thought he would make a wonderful teacher – evident by how he handled himself with the children in day care. I often think of that conversation.

During those early days especially, our family, friends, and church really came together for us. Eileen and Barbara came over bringing Scott's favorite chili. Jim, Mike and Megan were there and Kathryn was home on Christmas break from law school in California. Thinking back, everyone came together to create Team Scott. They helped with meals, transportation, cards, flowers, and visits. Our church even bought Scott an electric guitar and we got him lessons, all to lift his spirits. It was hard for Kathryn to be away during Scott's illness, but she would call frequently and make special trips home to see him. Scott could always count on a cousin if he was up for lunch at one of his favorite restaurants. It humbles me to think of the love and support that my family felt. This was all a living response to the question "WWJD" – what would Jesus do?

Gene

In the lives of most families there comes a turning point. A specific moment in time when life is altered from a course to which there is no return. Our moment arrived at around 6:30am on New Year's Day 2008. Chris and I were sleeping. Both of our, now college age children had spent New Year's Eve with friends. We were awakened by the phone which was mildly surprising given the day and hour. It was Scott. He spoke to his mom, she calmly listened then told him she would come and get him right away. After hanging up she told me Scott was not feeling well and he had some neck discomfort. She was concerned but certainly not panicked but thought it prudent to go to the emergency room and have him checked out. So began our odyssey.

That first day was a long one. Morning had stretched to afternoon; Scott was still in the ER. He had a chest x-ray and bloodwork done as well as a scan which was our first red flag, "only a precaution", Chris was assured. By now Kim was home and the extended family had been alerted that Scott's evaluation was becoming more complex. We went ahead with a New Year's get together at my sister's apartment but any celebration was becoming overshadowed by concern. Late in the afternoon it was determined that he would be spending the night in the hospital.

When we got word, Kim and I went over to the hospital immediately. We would have gone earlier but we expected him out with a simple explanation and a prescription. Worry was becoming heavier. We got to the hospital where mother and son seemed relatively light hearted and still expecting a benign result. In hindsight I am sure the doctor who attended to our son and had likely read his initial tests, did not share our optimism.

The next several weeks were a blur of anxiety and fear. The first hammer blow came with the news the next morning that Scott had a mass on his kidney, with this information we knew our boy was ill. Additional tests were scheduled with more waiting. During this time when not at the hospital, of course I was working because bills do not wait on illnesses. I would go for walks at lunchtime and during those seemingly endless few days while waiting for test results, I would walk into the local Catholic church and just sit and pray, but also ask God why us, why our son? There were times I just wondered whether there was a God at all. There did have to be at least a mustard seed of faith in my heart, I was after all, sitting in a church. Finally the results were in and the news could not have been worse. Cancer with a survival percentage in the single digits. How could this have happened?

It was not time for reflecting, there was much to get done. I was working but was also closely involved in Scott's care. My part was managing the logistics, picking up and dropping off prescriptions, running here and there while Chris tended to Scott. It was a frightening and depressing whirlwind. I remember waking one morning and while staring at the ceiling thinking, just for a second or two, of not having the strength to do this again today. Then I thought of my son and felt a pang of selfishness because the load on my back was nothing compared to the burden and fear my son was carrying. It was from that moment on that I was able to stay focused on the fact that this was his life and I was but a supporting character. The type of cancer Scott had was rare, aggressive, widespread in his body and very difficult to beat. The next year of his life would be dedicated to chemo, surgery, and radiation, while his disease would likely be held at bay for a time, it almost certainly would eventually recur. We were all devastated to the point of shock. There was no time to reflect because chemotherapy began immediately.

First Day of Chemo
Chris

Despite the poor prognosis, aggressive chemo was warranted to buy those two years and perhaps keep him going long enough for that miracle. After all, 10% did survive beyond that ominous two years. The chemotherapy and treatments were highly toxic and were scheduled to begin immediately. His treatment consisted of seven rounds, twenty four hours a day for one week, followed by two weeks off, then repeating the same schedule. On that first day, Scott and I were headed into Children's Hospital at Montefiore (CHAM) for his first round to begin at 7am. We are very nervous, not knowing what to expect. We signed in and waited to be called. We looked around at all the bald children with their weary parents not uttering a word to each other as we were trying to distract ourselves. Scott was listening to music on his iPod and I was pretending to be engrossed in a book.

Finally, they called Scott's name. We were led into a room where a nurse weighed and measured him. They also checked his temperature and blood pressure. So far, so good. Then the doctor and social worker arrived. They explained Scott's chemo protocol and told us what the side effects would be. We were told to expect a lot of nausea, diarrhea, and exhaustion. Then they gave our young adult son the consent papers to sign. Scott asked how long he would have if he didn't sign the papers. The answer was a few months. He signed. Next, the nurses brought him to the infusion room where the process was reviewed. The chemo would be administered thru his broviac line and at the end of the day, put into a backpack while still attached to his line, allowing him to go home at night. The chemo ran thru the night and we were to return at 7am. One full week on and two weeks off were considered a round. He was to have seven rounds.

When Scott left with the nurses, I realized that the doctor and social worker stayed with me to explain some sobering facts. The doctor told me that while they hoped to get Scott into remission, it was likely to come back with a vengeance. I stared at them in disbelief. Finally, I was able to ask them, "Why are we doing this then? What's the point if he's going to die anyway?" The doctor nodded his head and said that maybe it will give him more time and as we were to discover, time was the only hope that we had.

I remember walking out of the room and wandering down the hallway, my body shaking as tears rolled down my face. Gene was at work and I dialed his number. When he answered, in between sobs I told him what I just learned. Gene was shaken by this news but encouraged me to calm down before I see Scott. He would pick us up at the end of the day and we would talk more later. After about an hour, I felt better and went to see Scott. I sat with him in his cubicle, trying to stay positive. I decided not to tell him what the doctor said, I didn't want him to feel like giving up, he had just begun this journey.

I also met some other 'cancer moms' who showed me around, where to get coffee and where the chapel was. Each child had a different cancer and had different protocols. One thing all the moms had in common was that not one of us even considered that our child might have cancer. Even the very first time we brought them to the hospital because of neck or leg pain, we never thought of cancer.

Gene picked us up that night around 7pm, Scott wearing the chemo backpack. In the car, Scott's mood was good, indicating he didn't feel sick. When we arrived home I start to make dinner. Outside I hear a car beep its horn and Scott announced that he's going out with friends, chemo backpack and all and he leaves. Gene and I were so proud and happy for him. We even began to think "Maybe this won't be so bad." This thinking was short lived.

Gene

Shortly after diagnosis and the beginning of Scott's treatment's, I got a call from a good friend. He had scored two Super Bowl tickets through his family's connection with the New York Giants and was offering them to Scott and me. Excited and grateful as I was, I was not sure if Scott would be up to it. When I asked him, he said, "of course I want to go!" Luckily, the game fell between chemo rounds during a window of time when it would be safe for him to travel. With his doctors blessing, we were on our way to Phoenix to watch the Giants take on the undefeated Patriots. With the type of cancer Scott suffered from, the doctors wanted him to have as much opportunity as possible since I am sure they felt he likely would never get this chance again. We were on our way. Unfortunately, his illness also got on the plane for Phoenix.

Due to last minute planning, all direct flights were booked so we flew to Tucson, then drove the two hours to Phoenix. I rented a cherry red Mustang that Scott, a car lover, was itching to drive. He took the wheel for about an hour before fatigue got the better of him. We finally arrived at the hotel after a quick dinner at In n' Out Burger. I am sure the trip had been grueling on Scott but he had a day to rest before the game. On Saturday we just laid around for the most part, took a drive through Phoenix then checked in with Chris back home. In general, we thankfully had a very uneventful day. Before dawn on Super Sunday, however, I got a frantic call from Chris. Scott had a routine blood test taken before leaving and she had gotten word from Scott's medical team that his blood counts were low and they were concerned that exposure to the crowds at the game could be dangerous. I felt her worry was overblown given that his doctors had cleared him to travel. This mix-up in communication resulted in a somewhat heated exchange as I felt that base was already covered. Chris prevailed though and we headed to The Children's Hospital in Phoenix to run another series of blood counts. The nurses and staff were amazing, they got us in, drew my sons blood and had it analyzed all in less than an hour. Gratefully, the results did not raise any red flags and with adequate blood counts, we were off to the game.

We arrived at the stadium with plenty of time before kickoff. Security was tight with several layers of inspections. One required the removal of hats. Scott's hair was falling out from his treatment and it was quite patchy making it obvious that he was ill.

Yet he stoically endured this awkward moment, completed the security process, replaced his hat and we headed to our seats. I wanted so badly to comfort him but that would have only made it worse. We got to our seats, looking forward to the game.

The energy in the stadium was incredible. Everything about the experience was over the top. Alicia Keys was the pre-game and Tom Petty the half time entertainment. The game was a classic, the underdog Giants came from behind to beat the Pats on a last minute TD in what many called the most exciting Super Bowl ever. We had been invited to the Giants victory party, which under any other circumstances we would both have loved to attend, but Scott's stamina would not extend quite that far. We went back to our hotel, it had been a very long day and he needed to rest. We will always be grateful for the generosity of the Giants, my friend Jody for making it happen and another friend, Joanne from the Giants, who also helped to create this very special time for Scott and me.

The airline delayed our scheduled Monday return until Tuesday. When we finally did board our flight, it was clear that Scott wanted nothing more than to get back home. We were seated in the front of the main cabin by the bulkhead, Scott by the window with me next to him in the middle. A gentleman in his mid-forties sat next to me on the aisle. Scott was closing his eyes as the man and I were talking about the game, where we were from, simply engaging in small talk to pass the time. During the long wait sitting on the tarmac to take off, Scott eventually needed to use the restroom. When he was safely out of earshot the man asked compassionately "Is your son alright?" I told him no, quickly informing him what we were up against. He reached over and squeezed my leg in a show of support. What a nice thing for that man to do, kindness can be as big as Super Bowl tickets or a simple gesture of support. Had he once been through a challenge like ours or perhaps simply grateful he hadn't? I will never know. Scott returned to his seat; we were soon in the air headed back to NY. We sat in silence, each alone with our private thoughts… me, Scott and the man on the aisle.

What made that weekend so memorable was it was my time with Scott doing something special together. In the three years he had left we talked about it often. I had missed so much of his life trying to get mine together that memories like this were few and far between. That Super Bowl weekend turned out to be a memory never to be forgotten.

After our return from the Super Bowl and the initial shock wore off and Scott settled into his arduous treatment plan, our family was living in a new reality. We were all doing our best. The burden of course was heaviest on Scott and we wanted to give him something to look forward to, something that would bring him joy. Fortunately, we were able to splurge a bit. So, what does one buy a nineteen year old who is in such a difficult situation? A C230 Mercedes Sport of course! Nothing says joy to a young man like a hot set of wheels. My son was a great negotiator who knew when he had the advantage and he was in the catbird seat. It had to be a five-speed manual, a demand he came to regret as his body began to breakdown. He wanted something special. We looked at BMW, Audi, Acura and then we went to see a friend who managed the local Mercedes dealership. We gave him a few basic requirements and he walked us out to exactly what we were looking for as if it were just waiting for us. Silver, black interior, heated seats, sun roof, and it was a five-speed. Father and son instantly fell in love with that car! We went home that evening and told his mother that we had bought a car, certainly surprised by the brevity of our search, she exclaimed, "already!"

Scott loved that car! We lived on a busy street and had a small off street spot that was uncovered and not suitable for such a machine. Our good friend Dotty who lived down the street had garage space that was not being used and offered it to us free of charge. She was just one of the many angels who were there for us throughout this ordeal. Scott's treatment was rigorous to say the least. One week of around the clock chemo followed by two weeks off, then back at it. So, this only left him about a week in each cycle when he wasn't sick or in treatment. Then, off he would go radio blasting with just a little bit of normalcy amid the chaos of illness.

Chris

By the second month of treatment, Scott had a lot of anger. The chemo was difficult and he had to be hospitalized after the first round due to sepsis - a blood infection which although common, can be fatal. Because the chemo kills white and red blood cells, infection can happen usually about a week after the chemo stops. His temperature needed to be measured many times a day and if it reached 100.4, we would have to rush him to the hospital. Within a short time the fever could rise dramatically, leading to death. Needless to say, it is very stressful. Out of seven rounds of chemotherapy, he was hospitalized four times for infections. Because the chemo kills all the white and red blood cells, along with the platelets, transfusions are a frequent part of treatment. Transfusions were time consuming and often resulted in an overnight hospital stay.

Scott was angry because all of his friends were back in college and he was home. Not only was he home with his parents, but he was also very sick. He would go on Facebook and see all the fun his friends were having and when he looked in the mirror, he didn't recognize himself. Not a single strand of hair remained on his head; he didn't have eyelashes or eyebrows and his skin color resembled a piece of white construction paper.

I was trying to help him as best as I could, but he was taking his anger out on me. We were arguing a lot. The doctors wanted him to follow a special diet while on chemo, 'The Neutropenic Diet' which required all food to be cooked thoroughly. No fresh fruit or vegetables, no fast food or anything that may have been handled by anyone is permitted in order to prevent any exposure to germs, especially when his white blood cells are at their lowest levels. This sounded reasonable to everyone except Scott who would eat McDonalds and whatever else he wanted. While I would beg him to follow the doctors' orders, this was an area where he could maintain some control, so he felt compelled to do his own thing. So we would fight. I would have to clean his broviac lines; he wouldn't want me to, so we would fight.

Treatment was exhausting. We would have to be at the hospital by 7:00 am. Getting him into the car by 6:15 was no easy

feat. He was tired, cranky and angry. We wouldn't get home until
7:30 pm, he would try to eat, but the nausea would overpower him.
I would make him anything he wanted and I would cook whenever
he wanted. It could be 11:00 at night and if he thought he could eat
a grilled cheese sandwich and a milk shake I would make it. He
was losing weight and I was so scared he was going to die, I would
do anything.

How far would you go to help your dying child? Is there anything you wouldn't do? When Scott was first diagnosed, he asked his oncologist about medical marijuana. Although it was not legal in New York, the doctor confirmed that it would help with nausea, pain, anxiety and it would increase his appetite. As a mom, I didn't want the doctors giving my son the green light to use pot. When I expressed my concerns to his head nurse, she looked me straight in the eye and said, "Mrs. McMurray, your son's body is filled with cancer. If this helps, so what?"

Scott was 19 years old and had just gotten the okay from his doctors to smoke pot. All those years of "just say no" talks went out the window and now I was picturing my home resembling Woodstock.

By the time we got home from the hospital that day, Scott had made some calls to place an order. As he sat on his bed rolling a joint, he looked at me and smiled.

As of St. Patrick's Day, Scott had been receiving chemo for two months. We were heading home from the hospital after another long day of chemo when Scott began throwing up in the car. I pulled over about four times during the thirty minute drive. When we were close to home, Scott informed me that he didn't have any pot. I told him to call his friends.

"Everyone is out, it's St. Patrick's Day," he said. "I just want the vomiting to stop."

"There's got to be someone you can call," I said.

He picked up his phone and dialed again. I heard him ask for a small bag. I was relieved when he was able to find one. I told him we would stop to pick it up on the way home assuming we were going to one of his friend's homes. Instead, he directed me to the projects, a poor neighborhood in White Plains. I admit that I was scared. What if we got arrested? Or shot?

When we pulled up, a man approached the car. He was surprised to see me with Scott. The man handed us an envelope, we gave him the money. I was shaking. Never in my wildest dreams did I ever picture myself buying pot from a man in the projects. But I did and it was not the only time.

A few weeks before Scott's abdominal surgery which was the next phase of his treatment, he asked to go visit his college, SUNY Delhi, for a weekend. There was going to be a big fraternity party and he didn't want to miss it. At this point he had endured four rounds of chemotherapy and had been hospitalized several times for infections. His weight and energy level was low and I was worried about him driving three hours each way, but I also knew he should go. I offered to drive him. Not surprisingly, this did not make him happy. He wanted to drive, claiming he was perfectly fine. Unfortunately, I did not agree. Not only was I worried about his safety, but I worried about other drivers on the road. If he passed out while driving, he might not be the only one to be affected. Driving would become an issue between us and it created tension. If I felt he was not well, I had to make an unpopular decision. I hated having to sometimes insist he not drive, but I had to. Our compromise was that I would drop him at school and I would check into a motel in the area. I agreed not to text or call him and he promised to reach out to me if a problem arose. We would set up a time and place to meet the next day before heading home.

The day of the party arrived and Scott and I began our drive. We listened to Beatles and got McDonalds for the ride. When we arrived, I dropped him at the frat house and watched him go in. I noticed his thin body walking and pulling up his loose pants. I watched him adjust his cap so no one would see his bald head. I was so proud of him, especially knowing how uncomfortable it might be for him, where everyone was experiencing college life - a life that he had been relishing until cancer stole it from him.

I checked into the motel and watched TV. I brought a book and tried to concentrate on reading it. I was constantly checking my phone to see if he called or texted. It took all my will power not to reach out to him, but I didn't. A deal's a deal.

The next morning I arrived to pick him up. He was tired but happy. He told me he had fun and we headed home, listening to Led Zeppelin the entire way. When we got home, he headed straight to bed and slept the rest of the day. I didn't give this trip another thought, that is until I had a visitor soon after Scott's memorial. One of his fraternity brothers, Ben, stopped by for a visit and to bring me a fraternity shirt. As we sat at the kitchen table, I asked Ben for a 'Scott Story'. "Please, I asked, tell me something I don't know." Ben smiled. "Remember when Scott came up for a party, right before surgery," he asked. I nodded. Ben continued. "Well, we hadn't seen him since the winter break and we didn't know what to expect. Anyway, Scott walks in and when we saw him, our eyes filled with tears. He looked so different, he didn't have eyelashes or eyebrows. Scott sensed our sadness and said, "Guys, it's good, it really is. I'm driving a Mercedes and my Mom buys me pot!" We all burst out laughing! Of course, he was making this work for him! That's Scott, making the most out of any situation and making us laugh. I smile when I think of this. Yes, that's Scott, that's my son.

April 14, 2008

After four rounds of chemotherapy, Scott was scheduled for surgery on April 14, 2008, the anniversary of our first marriage. It was determined that the surgeon would remove a kidney and while they were in his abdominal cavity, if anything else needed to be removed, it would be.

A few days prior to surgery Scott was placed on a clear liquid diet. Doctor's orders. I had the refrigerator stocked with jello, broth and ginger ale. He was not happy. "Mom, I'm so hungry," he would say. I understood, but he was headed for abdominal surgery and he had to follow the doctor's orders.

We had to be at the hospital at 6am the morning of surgery and the night before, we were all a little nervous. At around 10pm Gene and I settled into bed. Soon after, Scott walked into our room, car keys in hand. "I'm going for a little drive, I need to clear my head," he said. We nodded and encouraged him not to be too late, we had to be up very early. Around midnight he returned and went to sleep.

We arrived at the hospital and waited anxiously for the surgeon to arrive. We had a new minister at our church and he came and prayed with us. Soon, the surgeon and orderlies arrived. We kissed Scott good-bye and Gene and I headed to the waiting room until the surgery was over. It was a long day. Our church nurse, Jennifer, sat with us for a bit, as did my parents. Over eight hours later the surgeon came to us. He said the surgery went well and along with a kidney, they also removed a muscle and some lymph nodes. Scott was in ICU recovering and we could see him.

I watched as Scott was wheeled into the ICU unit. He had been in treatment for four months and I could not believe how different he looked. He had lost a lot of weight, his complexion was the color of white construction paper and he didn't have a single strand of hair, not even an eyelash. He was sleeping. When I walked into his room, my eyes teared up at the sight of his bald head. I instinctively massaged his head and talked to him. I told him how brave he was and when he was feeling better, I hoped he could do everything he wanted to do. I went to his bedside and kissed his shiny bald head. I rubbed his head, his neck, his shoulders, then his feet. He did not awaken. As I was massaging him, I thought of Superman.

Superman was Scott's favorite superhero. As a little boy he would constantly wear his Superman pajamas. He wore them wherever we went. Some days, he would put a suit over them and tuck a pair of sunglasses in the pocket so he could be Clark Kent. He loved everything about Superman. He would lay on a chair, belly down, arms in front of him, and pretend that he was flying! One day when we were in the supermarket, there was a giant mess in one of the aisles, with broken bottles of mayonnaise, ketchup and other condiments strewn all over the floor. Ready for action in his trusty pajamas, three-year-old Scott marched up to the manager who was cleaning the spill and put his hands on his hips.

"This is a job for Superman!" he exclaimed.

Everyone smiled.

Scott was still sleeping but soon it was evident that there was a problem. He was losing control of his bowels and diarrhea was coming full force. As soon as I cleaned him up, another bout would come. Scott was beginning to wake up but he was very disoriented and I knew something was very wrong. I called a nurse and I wondered if maybe something happened in surgery, perhaps they left a sponge inside his body. I insisted that they x-ray him. They did and said everything was fine. But it wasn't, the diarrhea persisted. Scott continued to be in and out of sleep. Finally, I remembered something. "Scott, when you went for a drive last night, where did you go?" I asked. "Not gonna lie, I went to Burger King," he said. So much for the clear liquid diet! Approximately eight hours before abdominal surgery, Scott had a Whopper with cheese, french fries and a Coke!

Scott had endured approximately five months of treatment in which the chemo had ravaged his body. One of his kidneys had already been removed and now we were in the outpatient surgery area so he could have a bone marrow test. Scott was still on chemo but was also preparing for the next phase of treatment, a stem cell transplant. Needless to say, he was tired and very angry on this particular day. I was doing my best not to get on his nerves, but it was not easy.

Before the procedure, the nurse came in with the proxy paperwork. She explained to Scott that he needed to name someone who would make medical decisions on his behalf in the event that he could not do so himself. I fully expected him to say that his mother would be his proxy. Of course his mother would be his proxy!

"I want Junior to be my proxy," he said.

Junior was Scott's childhood friend. I told him to stop joking around, but he insisted that he was serious. I was getting mad.

"Seriously, Scott, these are legal documents."

He raised his voice and told me that he wanted Junior. I raised my voice in protest. The nurse asked me to leave and they took Scott for the procedure. I was in a daze. I couldn't believe he wanted Junior!

This is insane! I'm his mother! I thought.

I walked down the hall and the next thing I knew I was on the floor sobbing. I was a mess! One of the nurses called Scott's head nurse and informed her that I was on the floor. They put me on the phone.

"Chris, what's the matter? This is a simple procedure," she said.

In between heaving sobs, I sputtered out that Scott wanted Junior to be his proxy. She told me that was ridiculous and asked if I wanted to fix his wagon.

"Yes," I sobbed.

She told me to follow her lead on Monday.

Soon after, Scott was wheeled into recovery. My breakdown was over, and I felt better knowing there was a plan.

Proxy Junior, my aunt Fanny! I thought as I saw him. I was looking forward to Monday.

On the car ride home, Scott asked if I could stop at the deli and get him a sandwich. "Ask Junior," was my reply!

On Monday morning we returned to the hospital. When the head doctor came in, he got right to the point.

"I noticed that your friend's name is listed as your proxy."

Scott nodded.

"Is your friend Junior a stoner?" Scott shrugged.

"As long as Junior is your proxy, he cannot drink or smoke pot."

As Scott's proxy, Junior would have to make life and death decisions, so he had to have a clear mind. The doctor also informed Scott that Junior would not only need a beeper so he could be reached at all times, but he would also need to accompany Scott to treatment so he would be familiar with the treatment and medications. With that, Scott announced to the doctors that his mom would be a better proxy. It was great!

To raise awareness, we hosted the Friends of Scott McMurray Blood Drive at our church. Before Scott got sick, I never realized how important it is to donate blood. Transfusions are a major part of cancer treatment. Chemotherapy destroys blood cells, transfusions replace them. I cannot even count how many transfusions he had. We wanted the blood drive to be fun, so we had balloons and played music by The Beatles. The women from the church cooked his favorite foods and desserts. All of our family helped promote the event with their friends and acquaintances and it was a great success. We collected more than 160 units of blood. It was a great day and we continued to host a blood drive each year until we moved.

I waited until after the blood drive to do something I had wanted to for quite a while. I went to a tattoo parlor with Kim and got the Superman symbol emblazoned right over my heart. Let me tell you, it does hurt! When I got home, I showed Scott.

"Pretty cool," he said and smiled.

After recovering from surgery, he resumed chemotherapy. In June, he finished chemotherapy and was preparing for a stem cell transplant the following month. Between treatment and blood infections, Scott was hospitalized more than he was home that year. Our family worked well together. Kim came home from college every weekend to be with us. Our friends and family were always there, holding us up. Our common goal was making sure Scott was okay, that he was comfortable and that he knew he was loved. Each day we tried to give him some joy and peace through his daily struggle.

During his illness, Scott was still Scott and reported that he snuck out of the hospital one night for about an hour. Planning ahead, he called a friend and when visiting hours were over, he walked out with the crowd. His friend was waiting outside the hospital and they drove around and got fast food. I warned him not to do that again. Flashbacks of his high school years came to mind and I reiterated how bad it would be if he got kicked out of cancer treatment. I thought I had gotten through to him, but the next day we found out that he had done it again! This time he got caught by security and a nurse had to retrieve him. Thank God he didn't get kicked out of treatment, which probably never happens, but as Scott's mom, I worried about things like that. This escapade actually renewed his sense of life. He was happier, it was fun to him. Not so much for me!

Giving Scott joy and peace, however, came at a price and I learned the hard way how high that price could be. In March, Scott had been in treatment for a couple of months and I was showing signs of anxiety. I was busy taking care of Scott and I was having trouble sleeping. Nighttime was difficult, instead of relaxing, my mind kept focusing on worries about Scott and I was exhausted. One day I was with my friend Diana and I couldn't control my emotions. I began sobbing and blaming myself for Scott's cancer. After all, it is a DNA based cancer, I gave him that DNA, it's my fault. Logically I knew it wasn't true, but my heart, the heart of a mother, needed to blame myself. Why is that? There was no ready answer.

A few months later, I had a breakdown, it was scary. It started as an ordinary day, actually a good day. Gene had the day off and decided to play golf. Eileen had called and said she was off and was available if we needed her. Scott had completed another week of chemo. We were at the hospital the previous day for blood work and now he was sleeping soundly. It was mid-morning when the phone rang. I recognized the hospital's number, nervously I picked up. The nurse told me that they had the results of Scott's blood work and he needed to come in for a double transfusion and platelets. Not a shock, this happened a lot. I heard that Scott was awake, so I relayed the message. "I'm not going," he said defiantly. Soon we were arguing. I called the doctor and told him what Scott said and asked what I should do. "Call an ambulance when he passes out," was the response. I told Scott what the doctor said. Unfazed, he repeated that he was not going. I decided that I was not engaging in an argument and walked into the kitchen. I continually said in my head, "I'm not engaging."

I busied myself, made a cheese quesadilla (melted cheese is my comfort food) and went to my room, quesadilla in hand. Watching TV I was so proud of myself. No arguing, I just ate my snack. I looked at the clock at about 1:00 pm. The clinic closes at 7. He needed to go soon if he didn't want to spend the night. I just kept eating my snack. About a half hour later, Scott walked in my room. "I'll go, but I don't want you to take me," he said. "No problem, I replied, Aunt Eileen is off today, she can take you." He went back to his room. I was so proud of myself, no fighting. I called Eileen who would be here in 20 minutes. Looking at the clock, I realized he would have to spend the night, but decided not to tell him. I thought, "Wow! I will have a day to myself! I'll go on a walk, watch mindless TV, it's good." I heard a car beep and I told Scott his ride was here. Before leaving, he looked at me and said, "If I have to spend the night, it's all your fault, and I will never, ever speak to you again." Then he left. I stood there and all of a sudden my entire body started shaking. A cry and scream came from deep within me. I slid to the floor, hanging on the side of my bed. "It's not my fault!" I heard myself screaming. I could not stop the screaming and shaking and reached for the phone and called Eileen who was en route to the hospital. The screaming continued. "It's not my fault!" Eileen listened to my screams very patiently and told me that after she dropped him off, she would come back to my house. I was still hanging onto my bed screaming. "It's not my fault."

A little while later I heard someone on my porch. Thinking it was Eileen, I forced myself to answer the door. I was surprised to see Scott's friend, Mike. When Mike saw my face, he got nervous. "Where is Scott? Did something happen?" he asked. I began to speak but the shaking and sobbing began again. Mike just hugged me until I calmed down. I was still repeating that it's not my fault. Mike continued to hug me and told me that "Scott loves you, everyone does. He's just mad right now, but he loves you so much." After a little while I calmed down and wondered why Mike was here. "I left my skateboard in Scott's car, can I get it?" I nodded and thanked him for helping me.

Soon Eileen arrived and the shaking and sobbing continued. She brought vodka and poured me a drink to calm my nerves. I was exhausted, hysterical and I remember standing next to the wall, just sliding down to the floor. Eileen helped me to bed and waited outside for Gene to come home. Soon, Gene came home and Eileen left. Gene came into our bedroom and asked me to come into the living room to talk. I barely shuffled out, walking was such an effort and I was so tired. I sat on the couch and Gene sat on a chair approximately four feet away. Soon he spoke. "What did you say to Scott to upset him?" I was shocked by this question, struggling to find the words. My hand was behind my back and I felt the remote control. In one throw, I knocked him in the head! "What did I say to him?" I screamed. The shaking and guttural scream had returned. "Where have you been? You didn't even bring a phone!" I shuffled to our room, grabbed a blanket and his pillow and threw them at him. "Get out, when this is over, I never want to see you again!" I screamed. I slammed the door to my room and went to bed. At this moment I understood why the divorce rate is so high when you have a sick child. It's a pressure cooker, I got it. As I lay in bed, I was convinced my son was dying and I was getting divorced, again.

When morning came I heard Gene in the kitchen and I tried to get up but I couldn't. It felt like a pile of bricks were on me and I couldn't move. I closed my eyes. When I opened them again, I noticed two hours had passed. I tried again to get up and still couldn't. I told myself to get in the shower. I knew I would be all right if I could just get in the shower. I fell back asleep. When I awakened, the house was quiet. I knew Gene had gone to get Scott. Again, I tried to get up. It was so hard. I kept trying, finally getting out of bed. I was shuffling to the shower, still my entire body hurt. I really wanted to go back to bed but I knew if I did, this would be a serious breakdown.

After the shower, I made coffee and heard Gene and Scott come into the living room. I shuffled in. Scott looked at me, shocked and scared. I asked him how he was feeling, he said he was fine. I walked up to him, looking him directly in the eyes. "Let's be clear,

I said, you will never, ever blame me again for your cancer, understand? I know the cancer is in your body but you need to realize this is a family disease. We are all hurting." He nodded his head.

Although I was not happy to have gone through this, it was a defining moment for Gene, Scott, and me. From that moment on, we became a team. Our communication improved, we helped each other. We were in this together.

A part of Scott's treatment included a Stem Cell Transplant. A couple months prior to this, Scott had to give himself daily injections to boost his white blood count. The nurses showed him how to do this. He would gather up some of his stomach and inject the medicine. As a little boy, he always had a fear of getting shots at the doctor and I usually had to bribe him with McDonalds. I never witnessed Scott giving himself the injections. I would bring them to him, then leave the room. He would call me when he was finished. Honestly, I wasn't positive he was even doing this, but I knew he would have bloodwork done, and when his white blood count reached a certain number, they would be ready to be extracted. If his numbers weren't high enough, then he didn't do the injections and I decided to let the doctors and nurses deal with it.

The day arrived for blood work. His white cell count was satisfactorily elevated and they were ready for extraction. We made our way to another part of the hospital where Scott was hooked up to a machine for the six hour extraction process. His white blood cells were stored in a freezer waiting until they could be transplanted. The date for the transplant was set for the middle of July. It is actually a very difficult procedure and scary for the parents. Gene and I were told that there is a fatality rate of 20%. That means ten kids go in, eight come out. We decided not to share this information with Scott. He knew he would be hospitalized for a month and that I would be staying with him the whole time, that was enough information.

About a week before the transplant, Scott's friend Mike had a barbeque at his home. Scott got to see many of his friends and they had a good time. Gene and I were so appreciative for Mike and his family, it was just what we all needed to lift our worried spirits. A couple days before the transplant, Scott went out with some friends. Gene and I went out for burgers with some friends when I received a phone call from Scott. "Mom, I'm in a hospital in Connecticut, I broke my wrist skateboarding and they said I need surgery." Never a dull moment. I asked Scott to let me speak with a doctor or nurse. A doctor got on the phone and I told him that Scott is having a Stem Cell Transplant soon and his oncologist needed to be consulted. I called Dr. Gorelick and told him what happened. He said no surgery and no metal could be in his body because of the transplant. He agreed to call the doctor in Connecticut to work out the details. Gene and I headed to Connecticut to pick up Scott. When we arrived, Scott and his friends were at the hospital, Scott in a cast and in some pain. The agreement was that the cast would deal with the broken wrist but would have to come off during the transplant because the strong chemo would burn his skin if it was covered in a cast. We got home and Scott went to his room. I went to mine and I just shook with tears. My heart was truly breaking for my son. Couldn't he have a fun day with his friends? Hard enough that in a few days he would be hospitalized for a month, did he have to break his wrist too?

We had no sooner resolved the wrist issue when it became time to go to the hospital to begin the transplant process. There were two transplant rooms on the pediatric oncology floor set up quite uniquely to meet the special needs of a transplant patient.

Scott's room was divided in half - on one side was the patient's bed, a couch for me and a bathroom. On the other side was a room with a large window overlooking Scott's bed. A nurse was to be with him 24/7 to take care and closely monitor him. Any person who entered the room was expected to wear a sterile gown and face mask to ensure that Scott was not exposed to any germs, which could have been life threatening for him.

During the first couple days Scott was given anti-seizure medications that he tolerated fairly well. So far so good – we thought maybe this wouldn't be so bad after all. We spent most of the days watching and listening to John Lennon enjoying some home videos Yoko Ono had put to music of her, John and Sean Lennon. We loved this, especially a video featuring the song 'Mind Games' where John was seen walking thru Central Park, signing autographs and being silly. The videos were great, but I just cherished the fact that Scott and I could love the same music. I would lay in his bed next to him and we would talk and laugh, about the Beatles, cancer, anything.

One day when Scott was sleeping, I wandered down the hall to the social worker's office and asked them if they could help me find Yoko Ono's address. I wanted to write her a letter thanking her for putting together these videos. Within a couple minutes, address in hand, I was back in Scott's room composing a letter to Yoko Ono. I told her my son was a patient at Children's Hospital and was such a fan of John Lennon. Besides thanking her, I shared my gratitude that my 19-year-old son and I could bond over her husband's music. I mailed the letter, honestly forgetting about it. About a year later, I received a letter and a picture signed by Yoko Ono. In the letter, she asked how Scott was and that she hoped he was well. She sent the classic photo of her and John laying on a bed and autographed it. The day Scott received this he was not feeling well. I walked into his room with the letter and picture. After he read it he looked at the picture, then to me and smiled. "How did I get this?" he asked. I told him what I had done. He smiled so big, "so cool," he said. We found a frame and positioned the picture on his stand, right next to his bed. Scott and I often spoke about the note and picture. We knew that Yoko had a bad reputation, some people still believing that she broke up the Beatles. But to Scott and me she was a beautiful woman who made a very sick fan so very happy.

After the anti-seizure medications had done their job, the chemo drip began. Scott was given three different powerful chemo cocktails that would all work together. We were told the side effects would be very difficult. There would be a lot of nausea, vomiting, and open sores would develop from his nasal cavity to his anus. The chemo was precisely timed and every couple hours he was put in a bath and scrubbed clean to prevent burning. His bed sheets had to be changed frequently so his sweat on the sheets did not burn him.

For over a week, the chemo was administered. Every time he vomited, he screamed in pain because of the open sores in his throat. His suffering was unbearable for him and so painful to watch helplessly. Every scream ripped my heart open and I tried anything to ease his pain. I gave hundreds of foot massages, showed him cool music videos of John Lennon, anything to comfort or distract him. When finally, they were about to hang the last of the three chemos and the end was in sight, Scott was refusing to go any further. The doctors explained that if he were to give up at that point, all of this would have been a waste. Because the chemos work together, all three are needed for the required result. Scott continued to refuse, as he was over eighteen years old, he made his own decisions. The doctors explained how important the timing was and pressed for an answer. They left the room, leaving Scott and me to process this information. After a few moments of quiet, I finally spoke. I told him that I couldn't tell him what to do, this was his decision. I understood how difficult this choice was, but pointed out that he was almost done, only one last chemo round. If he didn't complete this, his chances of survival were pretty slim and we were holding out the hope that the transplant could give him time. I told him whatever he decided he would have my support. Soon the doctors returned and Scott told them to hang the bag, he would continue.

When the vomiting ended after the last round, Scott fell into a deep sleep. He slept like this for several days. I spent my time massaging him, reading and praying. Praying for Scott and me, that we both would have strength to get through this. Finally, it became time to replace the previously extracted white blood cells. What an anticlimax! They hung a bag of his white blood cells and they entered his body just like an IV. This took a couple hours and within a few days, Scott started to improve and the sores started to heal. Each day he got better until finally he could go home. It had been a month and he lost twenty pounds.

As he walked out of his room, the nurses stood up and clapped for him. He smiled and headed straight for the other transplant room where there was another boy about six years old, about to begin his transplant. This little boy and Scott had become friends during treatment. Scott would play his guitar and the little boy loved to be next to him. Scott looked in the other transplant room, saw his little friend, smiled and gave him a thumbs up. The little boy smiled and waved. Finally, we headed home. Scott had about a month to recover, then he had to have 28 rounds of abdominal radiation.

That month passed quickly and soon it was time to begin a month of daily radiation treatments. Beside his usual problems with his small intestine, the other side effects we were warned about included nausea, vomiting and exhaustion. His daily appointments were usually later in the afternoon so we were glad we didn't have to rush early in the morning to get there.

Many times as we were heading home, I would have to stop the car so he could vomit which was painful and embarrassing to Scott, so I would pretend it was no big deal. In fact, I just so happened to have a pail in the backseat. By now I had learned that it was better to not show any reaction, especially fear or sadness in front of him. If I was anxious, worried or just out of my mind scared, I walked away. It was not uncommon to find me crying on a bench outside his hospital room, but inside, I had it together. This was not an easy feat.

After completion of radiation, Scott was very sick. In fact, the only time he was out of bed was to use the bathroom. His weight once again plummeted and he was being fed by high calorie liquid nutrition through his broviac tube. He was miserable.

Soon it was Thanksgiving. We were planning on going to Eileen's home for dinner but Scott woke up that day so very sick, we soon realized that we needed a Plan B. I decided that I would make a little Thanksgiving for Gene, Kim and myself. If Scott was hungry, we would bring some food to his bed. I sent Gene to the store to buy a turkey breast but in his anxiety he bought a turkey, a ham and a duck! I made the trimmings and we had a quiet, but filling Thanksgiving. Scott slept pretty much the whole day and when he awoke we watched a movie together in his room. I remember people asking me if I was thankful that Thanksgiving, wondering if we said a blessing at our table. The answer to that is of course we did. We were thankful that Scott was alive and that we were all together and we also prayed for strength for all of us. I am sure there are many families who had that same prayer.

A few days after Thanksgiving was Scott's 20th birthday. He was so very sick and so very sad. Before heading into New York City, a few of his friends stopped by to wish him a Happy Birthday. He wished he could go with his friends but he knew that was impossible. My heart was breaking for him but I knew that I had to let him handle it. I couldn't fix this, I wished I could, I would do anything, but I couldn't. I heard him crying in his bed and I was crying in mine.

December 2008

Anticipating the end of Scott's treatment several months earlier, a family trip to Jamaica was planned to mark the occasion. Our trip was now imminent. We were scheduled to leave December 26th, the day after Christmas. We were so excited to be there for a week and couldn't wait to feel the warm sun. We did not take insurance out for this trip, didn't want to spend the extra money and besides, what could go wrong?

A couple of weeks before Christmas I heard Scott screaming in the bathroom. "Mom, come here, I'm yellow!" What? I walked in and standing in front of me was Scott and he was yellow! He looked like someone scribbled with a highlighter all over his body. Remember, I could not show fear, so I asked him how he felt. He reported that he did not feel sick, but the next step was to report in to his medical team. I called his doctor and got the instruction to come in immediately. As we were driving to the hospital I was worried that his liver was going to explode, right here, right now. Scott was anxious and put 'The Beatles' – his comfort music, on the stereo and soon we were talking about the music and singing along, then we arrived.

Because the hospital is a teaching one, many residents kept coming in to see the 'yellow boy'. Soon, his doctor walked in. He told us that before his radiation began, all the doctors discussed what could go wrong with Scott. The major concern was Scott's intestines, that the radiation could cause them to collapse. As a precaution, an ambulance was on call whenever Scott was receiving treatment to ensure a quick trip to Children's Hospital if needed, however, we had no prior knowledge of this. The doctor went on to say that no one, not one doctor considered severe jaundice. We were reassured that his liver would not explode but treatment was necessary. Scott could go home for now on medication, but we would have to come back a few times for bloodwork to make sure his liver was healing.

A couple days later I walked into Scott's room and he was shivering under the blanket. I took his temperature and it was 101 degrees; he had a blood infection. I quickly called his doctor and told him we were on our way. Gene was home. We helped Scott to the car and off we went – yet again, this time with added urgency as timing was everything. His fever was rising and the concern was that if sepsis set in before he was treated, it could be fatal. Finally we arrived and Scott was quickly given antibiotics intravenously and admitted. Usually the antibiotic course ran about a week. We were now thinking the Jamaica trip may not happen. I called Barbara and Eileen and told them that Scott has been hospitalized, he will be fine, but to be prepared that Jamaica may be cancelled. Of course, they could have gone without us, but I was happy when they said they wouldn't. After all, this trip was to celebrate Scott ending his treatment. Thankfully, the course of antibiotics ran without any problems and a couple days before Christmas he was released from the hospital. We had a wonderful Christmas and very early the next day we boarded a plane to Jamaica.

Jamaica was all that we hoped for but Scott was weakened by his year of treatments and could not fully enter into the activities. He did enjoy sharing a room with his cousins without anxious parents or aunts looking over his shoulder and particularly relished some of the activities on the beach. Snorkeling was out of

reach, but he enjoyed the boat ride and the highlight of the week for Scott and for all of us who had watched him endure the past year, was his triumphant ride on a jet ski!

As the New Year began, Scott had completed the major course of treatment but he continued to be dogged by the physical effects of that treatment. Scott's digestive problems continued until his death and I was worried that he would die from malnutrition. For some unknown reason, his small intestine stopped working. He was unable to digest and absorb any food. We tried everything, but his weight dropped to 121 pounds and at 6 feet 2 inches, he was dangerously thin. There would be quick fixes such as liquid feedings that went directly thru his broviac and bypassed the stomach. They were high in calories and Scott usually received them at bedtime. The problem was that the high sugar content could cause blood infections and it did. More infections, more hospitalizations, it was a vicious cycle. We had to get to the root of his digestive problems.

We went to GI specialists and Scott had to endure many embarrassing tests, such as colonoscopies and collecting stool samples. One test was particularly intriguing. He had to swallow a camera while he was fitted with a special kind of belt. The belt tracked the camera as it made its way thru Scott's digestive track and recorded its findings.

There was a span of about two weeks when we had to wait for the tests results. It was freezing in New York and Scott was showing signs of depression and anxiety. Most of his days were spent wrapped in a blanket, sitting next to the fire, watching TV. Gene and I wanted to lift his spirits so we decided that I would take

Scott back to Jamaica for a week. Might as well wait for tests results in the sun!

A few days later, Scott and I arrived in Jamaica. The next day we went parasailing. First, we hopped on the back of a jet ski, then boarded a boat, put on a harness and up we went! It was so beautiful and we loved it. At first I was nervous but Scott calmly pointed out different things to see and soon I relaxed and enjoyed the view!

When we got back to our room, Scott was exhausted. The excursion had worn him out and he slept for the most of two days. As the week went on, Scott was getting weaker and I was getting worried. Maybe Jamaica wasn't such a good idea after all. He was still having constant diarrhea and my heart broke every time I heard the bathroom door close. I saw that Scott was getting anxious too, because he wanted me to push our single beds together so he could lay next to me. When it was time to go home, he even suggested getting him a wheelchair at the airport. For Scott to suggest this, I knew he was really not feeling well, so that is what we did and we finally made it home.

A few days later we headed to the gastroenterologist for the test results only to hear that there were no answers, even with the fancy camera and another GI specialist was recommended.

A few weeks later, we are sitting in another GI specialist's office. After reviewing Scott's records and the myriad of tests he had been subject to, he reported that he was going to a GI conference in Europe and would like to present Scott's case. All the top GI doctors from around the world would be there and they can all discuss Scott's case. He was hopeful that they could find an answer. Scott and I left his office excited. Finally! All the top doctors! We will have answers!

Two weeks later Scott and I were anxiously sitting in his office, ready to hear the results. The doctor looked at us and said, "I presented the case. We think this is the price you pay for surviving treatment." My mouth opens, I was shocked. I must have misunderstood him, must be his French accent. I asked him to repeat this. He said it again, I was just as horrified. How can you say this to a 20 year old? Scott and I stood up to leave, still not believing what we had just heard. We got into the car and began a quiet ride home. Finally, Scott spoke. "Didn't think that was going to happen." I nodded, my eyes were filled with tears and I didn't want to speak because I was afraid I might cry. When we got home, Scott went to his room, closed his door and soon I heard the Beatles. I went straight to the phone and called his oncologist to tell him what happened. On the phone I was very clear and in control. As soon as I hung up, I went to my room, closed the door and cried.

For the next year we continued to seek help for his intestines. Finally we found some relief with prescribed pain meds. Usually pain meds can give a person constipation, but with Scott, it decreased his bouts from ten times a day to a manageable four. I have often wondered if it was the Burger King before surgery that caused all these problems. We will never know.

Despite all these issues, Scott was slowly building up his strength during 2009 and we were able to spend a lot of time together not focused on his illness. Our boy was growing up fast and his awareness and sensitivity to others was more and more evident. One morning during this year, I walked into Scott's room and he was watching an episode of Teen Mom. "Mom, do you believe this? This girl has a baby at 16 and her mom is helping her and she is so mean to her mother. Her mom is letting them stay there, helps with money and is always with the baby and all this girl does is scream at her." I nodded my head and told him that she just doesn't get it. He thought for a moment and said, "I didn't get it until I got sick."

"Well, aren't you glad you get it now at 20 years old, some people never get it," I responded.

We tried to give him as much confidence and independence as we could. He was unable to return to school that January, but we told him there was always Plan B and we encouraged him to think about what else he could do. During Scott's treatment, we learned that there are many organizations that donate services to terminally ill children. Some children can go on trips and some may get a special gift. Maybe it was because he would have had to admit that he had a terminal illness, Scott was very resistant to any special treatment. That is, until he heard about sky diving!

Sandee Candy was a fixture at Children's Hospital. Every Tuesday she would walk into the children's rooms pushing a cart filled with candy and toys. She owns and operates a nonprofit called "The Pinwheel Project." Through a variety of projects, both large and small, Sandee's goal was to make life a bit more pleasant and peaceful for those facing some of the worst challenges they could ever imagine. I looked forward to Tuesdays. Not only did I get chocolate, but I got to know a caring person who brought smiles to children and their parents. It was Sandee who suggested sky diving. She knew of a place and told us the Pinwheel Project would pay for his jump. Scott was very excited.

The day of his jump arrived. Gene and I drove Scott two hours north to "The Ranch". As we got closer, we were able to see the parachutes in the air. Always with a song appropriate for the occasion, Scott played 'Free Falling,' a song by Tom Petty on his iPod as we pulled in. Scott attended the pre jump lesson and met the instructor to whom he would be attached in his first tandem jump.

Soon, Scott boarded a plane and took off. Watching nervously, Gene and I suddenly spotted his parachute, he was flying! After he landed, he walked over to us with an excitement we had not seen in over a year. He loved it and wanted to enroll in the classes, hoping to one day jump by himself, without an instructor. Before we left, Scott was given a video of his first jump.

When we got home we looked at the video. There was Scott flying, but what we saw that was by far even more amazing, was his smile. We had not seen that for quite a while, but there it was and it was beautiful!

The next day I enrolled Scott in sky diving classes. One or two times a week we would drive to The Ranch. I would sit and read a book while Scott was in class. Sometimes the classes would last for hours and sometimes I would get bored waiting for him to finish, but I was truly grateful to see him happy again. The car rides were always filled with music, talking, laughing and junk food. Scott eventually jumped by himself, in fact, over the course of a year, he jumped 15 times! The skydiving instructors at the Ranch were very understanding of Scott's illness and went out of their way to make sure that he had a special experience there. A wonderful surprise for Scott was receiving as a gift, a video of his first solo jump which included his exiting the plane, descent and landing. This video was shared with all of Scott's family and friends at his memorial service as a fitting testament to his zest for life.

Early in 2009, Scott began to plan a cross country trip to California with his friend Mike. Knowing what Scott had been through over the last year and after the difficult time he had in Jamaica, this was a very worrisome proposition. Wanting to encourage his enthusiasm, alternative options such as sticking to the East Coast and perhaps going to Florida were suggested, hoping he would choose a less strenuous alternative. I told him that California was the mecca of road trips and suggested he might want to work up to that. His reply, "Mom, I don't have time for that," stopped me in my tracks. We decided to put the decision in the hands of his doctors, confident that they would discourage this venture. To our surprise, they began problem solving how to get him his medication as he travelled across the country. A plan was developed where we would mail his medications to PO Boxes

across the country. Not only would that solve the medication dilemma, it would also give us the opportunity to connect with him about twice a week to let him know where to pick up his meds. So, in June, the entire family launched him on his adventure with an extended family barbeque!

They were gone about three weeks and when they returned, we stood on our front porch and clapped as they pulled into the driveway. We were so happy and so was he! We may never hear many of the stories from that trip, but he treasured the experience and the memory. He slept for a week, but it was worth it. And as far as we know, the most drama was a couple speeding tickets.

In September 2009, I was driving Kim across the country to begin a new job in New Mexico when I got a call from Gene.

"Scott was arrested last night."

"Arrested? For what?" I asked.

I was surprised because Scott had been very sick, rarely leaving the house over the last several weeks. Since returning from his cross-country jaunt, Scott started complaining of shoulder pain. He was also sleeping more. I spoke with his doctors and we concluded Scott needed physical therapy. He needed to build up his muscles to get stronger and his small intestine was still not functioning properly.

Gene explained that Scott woke up feeling very sick, so he called a friend to ask about getting some pot. The friend offered to make some calls. He was able to find some through another friend and offered to pick Scott up to get it. When they arrived at the friend's house, he ran outside to make the delivery. The entire exchange took only a minute, but a cop had witnessed the transaction and pulled them over to confront them. The policeman was unsympathetic to Scott's illness. He handcuffed the boys and brought them to the police station where they were tethered to a pole. The friend who had supplied the pot was brought in with the other boys. Scott did not have any identification with him and could not be released until Gene arrived. The next day, Scott was very sick. He had a high fever, chills, and more diarrhea. On top of complications from the cancer treatment, he now had the flu. I was so angry. I know he must have gotten sick from being at the police station and that illness hung on for about three weeks.

Soon, a court date was set. We brought a doctor's note detailing Scott's medical condition and his prognosis. In the note, the doctor had also stated that marijuana helped manage the symptoms from his complications. I did not show Scott the note, worried that seeing the prognosis in black and white would be too upsetting.

As we were waiting for the judge to call him, Scott grabbed the note and read it. I didn't want to make eye contact, but out of the corner of my eye, I could see him read it, shake his head, and hand it back to me. He then put his head on my shoulder.

When his name was called, Scott approached the bench. The judge read the note, gave Scott a once-over and told him not to smoke pot. We paid a fine and went home. Scott lay in my bed and fell asleep. Still unable to control my anger, I went outside to get some air. As I sat on the porch, I thought about how much I hated this city.

Really, he had to be arrested?

I decided to go for a walk, stomping my way through the first half mile.

The following January, Scott returned to school. He was still very thin and weak, but he wanted to go back. Scott wasn't the greatest student, in fact, he returned on academic probation. I reminded him that he needed a 2.0 GPA to stay in school.

"No problem, Mom," he said. "I got a 1.2 without even trying."

He was totally serious! While he was sick, he would tell me that if he ever got the chance to return to school, he would do so well, adding that you don't appreciate something until it is gone. So he went back to school, but it was a struggle to stay on campus seven days a week. On Fridays, I would pick him up along with his laundry at noon. While home, he would rest and eat. On Monday mornings we would be in the car by 5:45 a.m. to get him back to school by 9:00 a.m. We did this the entire semester, with the exception of a couple weekends. He started to talk about becoming an early childhood teacher, which is what I always thought he would be. He had always been the Pied Piper among the little children at Chris's Kids Day Care, so this was the next logical step for him. Scott's returning to school this semester was a big accomplishment in itself and we had no expectations about grades and just appreciated that he could return to a somewhat normal life and hoped he could get that 2.0 so he could stay in school. However, when his grades for the semester were posted, he did so well that he was eligible for the teaching program. I burst out crying.

That summer, he went to Bonnaroo with some friends. While he was there, he called me and said his neck hurt again.

"It's that same pain, Mom," he said.

I told him not to worry, that maybe it was anxiety. I wanted him to have fun, he deserved that.

When he returned from Bonnaroo, I took him to see his doctors. They prescribed physical therapy for his neck and also his shoulder, which was giving him some pain. The rest of the summer Scott did well. He was going to physical therapy a couple times a week and he was seeing his friends. He was also looking forward to returning to school. He was beginning to look better, was gaining some weight and his hair was getting thicker.

Also, during that summer, he was offered a part time job from an acquaintance at the church. A woman who gave voice lessons needed someone to help with her elderly husband when she was working for a couple hours two to three times a week. Scott's job was to make him lunch and keep him company. This man was a retired doctor whose specialty was gastroenterology and he had begun to experience some health issues. Scott was excited about the job and making some money. I had my own fantasy about this job. I had visions of Scott and the doctor developing a strong bond based on hours of meaningful discussions. They would learn important life lessons from each other, an old man and a terminally ill young man. Also, being that he is a former expert in GI, I expected that he would solve all of Scott's intestinal problems! I can even hear music playing as I think back on this scenario.

When Scott visited the doctor, sometimes he rode his bike or skateboard or sometimes I drove him, depending on how he felt. He was always happy to go and was in a good mood when he returned. Several weeks went by before I asked him what they talked about. Scott thought about this and told me they talk mostly about sports and they watched TV. This was not sounding like *Tuesdays with Maury* to me. Then Scott said, "You know Mom, getting old is very hard. He can't do a lot of things anymore. He can be cranky and sad but I understand. He has it so much harder than I do." Then he walked away. I am blown away from what I just heard. I went to the front porch and burst into tears. Scott thinks an eighty something year old man has it harder? This man lived a wonderful life, a life filled with knowledge, travel, expertise, marriage and family. My son is twenty-one years old and fighting to live. The odds of Scott surviving are small. He may never complete college, have a career, a marriage or a family. Yet, he thinks the doctor has it worse! Wow! I am still amazed when I am reminded of this. Such compassion, such empathy. Maybe Scott and the doctor didn't have a *Tuesday with Maury* moment, but I sure did.

One day when Scott got home from the doctor he told me he got mugged. He was walking home and a couple of men told him to empty his pockets, so he did. I was shocked and so angry. I told Scott to get in the car so we could go to find them. I didn't care who they were, how big they were, even if they had a weapon. I wanted to get them! Scott started to laugh, he said he's picturing me trying to beat up his muggers. I started to laugh too. I asked him why he was not upset. Smiling, he took off his shoe and pulled out a twenty dollar bill. "I only had a couple of dollars in my pocket, they didn't ask me to take off my shoes!"

At the end of August we drove him back to school. He was so excited. When we dropped him off, Gene and I looked at each other and said, "maybe he'll be the one to beat this." He had passed two years already, we were so hopeful.

Three weeks later Scott called. His thigh was hurting. He was in a hospital near his school. His voice was shaky as he held back tears. These doctors told him that his cancer was back. I tried to reassure him that we couldn't think this way until we spoke to his oncology team. He wanted to be alone that night, but we would be there in the morning. We called his doctors and told them to expect us the next day. We planned to drive up to Delhi, discharge him from that hospital and bring him to his doctors in the Bronx.

That night, Gene and I tossed and turned. He couldn't be sick again. He just couldn't. He looked better than he had in two years. This just couldn't be. Still unable to sleep, Gene and I began the drive to Delhi around 5:00 a.m. When we arrived, Scott looked exhausted. I told him that we were going to see his doctors. I wanted this trip to be as stress free as possible, so I had blankets and pillows in the backseat and the Beatles music playing. We stopped and got some snacks. I didn't even argue when he wanted candy for breakfast.

When we arrived at Montefiore, the doctors took a look at his X-rays and ordered more tests. They told Scott to try not to worry. Easier said than done. Over the next few weeks, Scott had CAT scans, an MRI and a PET scan. He became very anxious and we worried he might have a breakdown. He was struggling to come to terms with the fact that he was likely sick again, what might happen and how he might be able to finish school. We tried to keep the mood at the house as positive as we could. I cooked his favorite foods, we watched movies and we always had a fire in the fireplace. I gave him plenty of foot massages and we just talked.

The house became a sort of cocoon, we rarely left and were waiting for the doctors to call with the test results. I knew that when the results were in, our lives could be forever changed, so until then, we were good in this cocoon.

Soon, the doctors called and wanted us to come in to discuss the test results. The next morning, we were in the waiting room, anxiously waiting for them to call us in. Finally, it was Scott's turn. First was the usual routine in which blood pressure, temperature, and weight were taken. When the nurse, who was one of our regulars was sniffling, I asked if she had a cold. She shook her head no. Looking back on it, I am sure she knew what we were about to face. Then the room began to fill up with his doctors, nurses, some interns and then I saw the social worker. Her presence told me that we were about to hear the worst possible news. Now I was really petrified.

Dr. Gorelick looked at Scott, said that the test results were back and it was not good. There was a recurrence of the primary cancer and at this time, there was no treatment or cure. Scott asked how long he had. A few months was the answer.

The car ride home was very quiet, all you could hear was Scott and me sniffling.

When we arrived home, Scott looked at the house, then turned to us and said, "This will not be a sad house."

The tone was set.

I went for a walk to clear my head. Scott went on his computer and Gene called Kim with the news. She had recently moved back to Philadelphia, in part to be closer to Scott. When I returned, Gene said he was going to Philadelphia to bring Kim home, a decision Scott objected to, noting that he didn't want to make a big deal of this. I had to respond that it really was a big deal.

Then Scott asked me to take him to Best Buy to get PlayStation 3.

"You're going to milk this, aren't you?" I said.

He smiled.

Along with the PlayStation 3, we also bought two games.

"Would you like a two-year warranty?" asked the salesgirl.

"Oh, I don't think I'll be needing that," Scott said.

I don't know if it was nerves or shock, but we both giggled at this.

"Guess what I just did?" Scott said after we left the store.

I looked at him blankly.

"I just stole a pack of gum. I've always wanted to do that!"

I told him I had enough things to worry about and coming up with bail money was not one of them!

For the next couple hours, it was just Scott and me in the house. This was good, it gave us an opportunity to talk about the recurrence. I made a fire and we ordered sushi.

"When I'm gone, I want you to have another baby," Scott said.

"No freaking way," was my answer. "I'm not doing homework when I'm in my sixties."

"You have to, it's my dying wish," he said in typical Scott fashion.

"Think of something else," I answered.

I then told him how lucky I was to have an amazing son and a wonderful daughter. Soon our sushi arrived and we watched a movie. It was hard to focus on the movie, I kept thinking that my son was going to die. When the movie was over, Scott could see the tears in my eyes.

"Scott, I have to ask you—"

"Mom, I had a great childhood, you were always there for us. We laughed a lot in this house."

That was all I needed to know. My job of raising him was over and my new job was beginning. I now had to let him die. I had to prepare him to die, on his terms, so in the end, he would be at peace knowing how much we loved him. I don't think there is anything harder for a parent to do.

I know many people question their faith during crises, asking how God could let this happen. I never felt this way. I know God did not give Scott cancer. Cancer is not selective, anyone can get it. Scott knew cancer was random. He also knew how rare it was. "Guess I'm the lucky one," he would say sarcastically. That's how he looked at it.

Scott's oncology team had discussed with us the various options for his care as he became weaker and the disease ravaged his body, but there wasn't much to discuss. Soon after the diagnosis, Eileen came to visit. As she walked into his room she said, "I have always loved you," to which Scott replied, "I have always loved you too." This reminded us how important it was for Scott to be able to spend as much time with family and friends who loved him. In home hospice was by far preferable to hospital or in-patient hospice care. He would still be considered a patient with his oncology team, but also with a team from hospice. I would be his primary caregiver, but hospice would also send us a nurse to monitor him. His friends and family could come anytime they wanted and he could come and go as he pleased, for as long as he could.

When the hospice team first came to meet Scott, they brought a lot of paperwork. One of the items was a consent for cornea donation. As Kim and Scott were growing up, the subject of organ donation was one we often talked about. We all felt that when we had no further need for our organs, why not donate? We talked about how this could make someone else's life better when we're gone. Of course, this was all hypothetical, never imagining we would so soon be faced with this decision. Until now. Now this is real. I brought the paper to Scott and sat beside him. Even though his body was ravaged by cancer, his eyes, his corneas were healthy. I told him to think about it and to let me know. I left the paper with him. About a half hour later, he found me in the kitchen and sat down. "I signed the papers," he said. "Do you think they will get my speck of gold?" he wondered. I told him I hoped so. He had beautiful eyes with a very distinct speck of gold. He handed me the papers and I put them in an envelope for hospice when the time came. This brought it all home. This was real, it was really happening.

At first, Cheryl, his nurse, came once a week. As the disease progressed, she would come more often. Toward the end, Cheryl came every day. She would check his blood pressure, take his temperature, listen to his heart and lungs and monitor his pain levels. She would stay for about 45 minutes each visit. She instructed me on how to give the pain meds, starting with pills, then pain patches, and when he could no longer swallow solids, liquids. Hospice also provided a massage therapist once a week. Before she came, I would light a fire and play music. Scott loved these massages and it did help ease his painful bones. Another benefit of Hospice was that all Scott's medications were delivered to our front door. No more waiting in lines at the pharmacy; I could always be with Scott. They also provided me at no cost grief counseling for a year. This was instrumental in helping me navigate this new life, and the 'firsts' of everything, birthdays, holidays, and so many painful days that are a part of everyday life.

Cheryl was a former nun with a great sense of humor and a contagious laugh. Scott connected with her; we all did. One time, she left Scott's room laughing. He had told her that dying is so [expletive deleted] boring! That was pretty funny.

Gene

During Scott's treatment there were a lot of drugs around our house. Some of them were the type that under normal circumstances were not safe for a person like me to be around. Early on, there was marijuana that Scott used in an attempt to offset the effects of his chemo treatments. It helped not only with nausea, but also stimulated his appetite. Sometimes he smoked a couple of joints a day. That familiar sweet odor was wafting through the house regularly. Toward the end, when pain management was the goal, the highly addictive oxycodone was in abundant supply. Chris always managed the pain meds and probably kept them hidden, not knowing if they would be a temptation to me. There were times though, when Chris was just not available and it fell on me to dispense the meds.

As Chris and I discussed topics for our story, she thought that it was important that I address the drugs and how I felt about their presence in the house and how I dealt with it. The simple answer is that it was never an issue. I know that there was some worry by the people closest to me, who lived through the hell of my active addiction, that my proximity to these substances could be a danger. My program tells me that if my motives are correct, I should not fear any situation and easing the pain of my son at that time was my only motivation.

There was a distraction that, for me, was far more difficult to deal with. The effect of our son's illness and our family's plight, was profound not only on us, but for many friends and acquaintances. As I mentioned earlier, almost everyone wanted to help. We will forever appreciate that. On several occasions and from more than one source, we were subjected to unsolicited advice. There were some who knew of a doctor with the 'miracle cure' that Scott just had to see. Others offered advice on the merits of a certain extract or other natural concoctions that would somehow melt away the cancer. The annoying part of this advice was the urgency and an insistence of a better way to a cure than the one, after much counsel and prayer, we had chosen. Truthfully, this is a very, very personal decision. When a patient and family embark on a treatment plan, it requires total commitment, laser focus. We had decided on and put our trust in a team of physicians who laid out Scott's treatment plan. There was no time or energy to try a regimen of asparagus extract shakes, which was suggested by the boss of somebody's brother in law.

I do understand they were only trying to help. There was another, much smaller group of both friends and family who just disappeared. I know there have been times in my life when I have been absent from a loved one's time of need and it has forever altered that relationship. A phone call is always better than no call and the excuse that "I didn't want to bother you in your difficult time," always rings hollow.

Chris

Around the middle of November, Scott asked for one more family vacation. His first thought was the Grand Canyon, but I knew this would be too strenuous. I suggested Las Vegas. He was of legal age and Cirque du Soleil did a show called *Love* with music from The Beatles. It would be perfect. A few days later, we flew to Vegas. The show was amazing, but looking at Scott, knowing he would die soon, was so painful. Tears filled my eyes but I wiped them away so he wouldn't see them. I knew that I was his biggest worry. "I worry about you the most," he would tell me.

Thanksgiving was a bittersweet holiday this year since we knew it would be Scott's last and family members from everywhere came to be part of this special day. We celebrated in our family's traditional way and we all had something to look forward to the following day as Eileen and Jim had gotten tickets for all of us to see a performance of Cirque de Soleil at Madison Square Garden. We rented a van instead of taking the train as Scott's bones were frail and his stamina was limited. We started the evening with a pizza party at Jim's Manhattan apartment before going on to MSG. The show was wonderful, Scott loved it, but for the rest of us, the highlight of the evening was watching Scott jump on the banister of the down escalator, slide down, fly a little in the air, land perfectly then continue walking like nothing happened. We all stood there, mouths open and began to laugh. It was so amazing. It was so Scott.

Now it was December and as Christmas was approaching, I knew that I had to decorate the house, but I was dreading it. How could I look at these ornaments, many of which were handmade by Scott and Kim or purchased on family vacations? How could I smile and remember happy times when my son was dying? Then a friend called. She was going to buy her tree and offered to get us one too. A few days later, a tree appeared on our porch. That is Christmas. We set up the tree and Kim and Scott began to decorate it. They were happy remembering all the good times each ornament reminded them of. What had begun as a dreaded endeavor soon turned into such a joyous time. After the tree was decorated, Gene and Kim went to pick up Chinese food. Scott and I lay on the couch admiring our beautiful tree. He began to sing. I had never heard this song before, but it was about a passing. As I listened, I began to get choked up. He was happy right now. He was content. He was dying. We knew that this would be our last Christmas together as a whole family, but it was not a sad house. We were grateful to have each other, our families, our friends, we knew this. That Christmas was so beautiful.

In January, Scott was getting visibly weaker. It was hard for him to walk and his breathing was more difficult, but that did not stop him. He went to Florida with some friends and to a concert with his sister. The end of January was the last time he was able to leave the house – but in true Scott fashion, that trip was for one last joy ride up 684 with one of his best friends in his beloved

Mercedes. Over the next month's, Scott still enjoyed spending time with his friends who were such an important part of his life and saying good bye to them all at the right time.

Gene

That car made a lot possible by way of freedom for Scott during the journey through his illness. He was able to travel cross country after treatment had ended and he was NED (no evidence of disease) with his dear friend Mike. A trip I know little about beyond the fact that they both got speeding tickets. Later on he was able to drive back to college, although the rigors of a long drive were taxing on a body ravaged not only by disease, but treatment as well. He didn't always take his car. As Scott came home from school most weekends, usually Chris would make the six hour roundtrip in our family car. Every so often I would go pick him up at school in the Mercedes and he would drive for a half hour or so, then he would ask me to take over because he needed to close his eyes. When the cancer returned, that car was his refuge, while he was still able, he would just go for a drive to be alone. At the very end, shortly before he was bedridden and seldom left home, he convinced his friend BJ to go for one more drive. They conspired to find the keys and took off. They were only gone for an hour or so but these two close friends had one last road trip. Details again unavailable, except that they returned safe and sound.

There were periods when he got to drive his car often, but there were also many long stretches when he could not. We did our best to make sure Scott never drove if he was too weak or under the influence of pain meds. It was heartbreaking to deny him this one simple pleasure, but the safety of everyone else's family out on the road was paramount. During one of our trips back from his college as I drove, I looked over at him, he had a reflective look on his face and I asked him "What's up?" He smiled just a bit and said to me, "Dad, you know, driving this car just makes you feel good." To which I replied, "Yes bud, it does." It was so worth it.

Chris

One night Scott and I were in the living room watching a movie. A fire was lit and his tired body was stretched out on the couch under a blanket, his feet on my lap and I was massaging them. When the movie ended I stood up to go to bed. Scott said he was staying up, so I leaned in to kiss him goodnight. As my face neared his, he grabbed my face with his hands and looked me intently in the eyes. "I love you," he said with short labored breaths. I kissed him and told him that I loved him too. He smiled and I went to my room. I closed my door, sunk to the floor burying my face in my shirt so he couldn't hear my muffled cries. My son is dying, my heart is breaking. How am I going to do this? How?

The month of February brought another new challenge for Scott. His breathing was becoming more and more labored. One of his lungs had stopped functioning and an oxygen machine was needed. When it was delivered, Scott was very distressed, insisting that he would not use it. Into the closet it went – but a few days later he asked if the oxygen machine would prolong his life. After learning that it could not, but would make him more comfortable, he agreed to try it and it did help quite a bit!

Each morning, I would get up and start a fire. If he felt strong enough, Scott would come into the living room and lie on the couch. While we watched TV, I would massage his feet.

"We have all gotten even closer since this," he said while laying there one day.

I agreed.

"That's a plus," he said.

I nodded and smiled, he was right. It was a plus. Our family was facing the biggest trauma one could face and we were stronger for it.

"Scott, do you wish you would have died during treatment?" I asked him one day. We were laying in his bed, watching a movie. I wanted to know if he felt like the treatment was a waste of time or if being cancer-free for a year and a half was a tease. Scott thought about this question. He was confined to bed, his body broken and his organs were shutting down. He now used the oxygen machine 24 hours a day.

"I've thought about that," he said. "No, I'm glad I didn't die during treatment. I got to do a lot of cool things and now I get to spend my time with the people I love the most."

I was filled with so much love, pride, and admiration for him. I grabbed his hand and kissed his cheek. I told him that even though he never graduated from college, he did become a teacher. He taught us so much about life and death. I also told him that I was so happy that he was mine.

By March, Scott was unable to walk. He had no muscle tone and only very infrequently did he make it to the couch. He was mostly in his bed or mine. To move him, we put him on a swivel chair and wheeled him around. Many nights, either I slept in his bed with him or he slept in my bed with me, usually depending on his day. One night when I was in my bed and he was in his, he called out for me. I stumbled into his room.

"I'm not dreaming, but a boy was in my room," he said.

I asked him if he was afraid. He shook his head. I asked him if he recognized the boy, he thought maybe it was a little boy he knew from the hospital. He soon fell back to sleep.

About a week later Kim and I were watching a movie in Scott's room.

"There's a boy on my bed," he said.

"Do you recognize him?" I asked.

"No, but why are they coming to me?" he wondered.

"I think they are here to tell you that it's all right and not to be scared."

A few days later, Scott was laying in bed, crying.

"What's the matter, bud?" I asked.

"I'm scared dying is going to hurt," he said.

I lay down next to him and wrapped him in my arms.

"It won't hurt," I promised. "You will just go to sleep. Your body will feel so good—no more pain—and you will fly so fast to Heaven."

He liked that and soon calmed down, then fell asleep in my arms. While he lay there, I cried quietly.

Scott was sleeping more. He could not walk and his breathing was very labored, even with the help of the oxygen machine. One night in the beginning of April, Scott was sleeping in my bed. He was closest to the wall with his oxygen machine next to him on the floor. Approximately three feet from the foot of the bed was a big-screen TV. Gene was sleeping in Scott's bed when a strange sound awakened him. He got out of bed and found Scott sitting on the toilet. He woke me up to show me, there was Scott, asleep, sitting on the toilet, not attached to his oxygen machine. We approached Scott carefully so as not to startle him. We put our hands on his shoulders and back to steady him because *he had no muscle tone and could not walk*!

We gently asked him if he was okay.

He nodded.

We asked him if he needed help.

He nodded.

We got the swivel chair, placed him on it, bringing him back to bed. We reattached him to the oxygen machine. Scott soon fell asleep. I looked around. There were blankets on the floor and the oxygen machine was still next to the bed. How had he done this? I usually heard every sound he made. How could he have removed his oxygen tank, gotten out of bed, climbed over strewn blankets, maneuvered around a small corner and walked to the bathroom, all without me hearing any of this? Confused but exhausted, I fell asleep.

The next day I talked to Scott about the incident. I explained that if he needed help during the night, he had to wake me, because if he fell and had broken a bone, he might have to be hospitalized and then I couldn't take care of him at home.

"I don't remember any of that," Scott said.

With every fiber of my being, I know Scott was somehow carried that night. Was it by angels? Maybe. Or maybe it was deceased family members. I don't know. I just know he was carried.

During this time, Cheryl was coming daily to check on Scott. I asked her how long she thought he had. Her answer was a couple of weeks. After Cheryl left, I lay down next to Scott. He had overheard my conversation with Cheryl.

"Only a couple of weeks?" he asked.

I nodded.

"Please get me pen and paper," he said.

I did and Scott proceeded to tell me how I was to distribute his most prized possessions. I wrote everything down as instructed, put the paper on the shelf, and lay down next to him, holding him and telling him what an amazing man he had grown up to be.

About a week later, Scott and I were in his room, listening to music. I was again giving him a foot massage.

"Mom, what do you think Heaven will be like?" Scott asked.

"I think it will be such a great place. You won't have any more pain and your body will feel so good and you will fly so fast to Heaven. In Heaven, you will be able to do whatever you want. You will be very happy. Also, you'll get to hang out with all the famous people you admired, like John Lennon."

"John Lennon's not going to want to hang out with me," Scott said.

"Of course he will. He'll probably thank you for being such a huge fan," I said.

Scott just looked at me.

"In Heaven, there are no cliques. Everyone hangs out with each other," I said.

"You make it sound so good," Scott said.

"Because it is so good." I then reminded him that he had read a lot of stories about people having near death experiences and not one had ever come back saying Heaven was horrible!

We both laughed. I told him that he would also see Grandma Phyllis and Grandpa Eugene. "How will I recognize them?" he asked. " Well, I said, they will be waiting for you and when you see them, you will have the feeling of just knowing," I said.

After this conversation, I always used the word *fly* instead of *die*. When I knew that he was hanging on for me, I would tell him that it was okay if he wanted to fly tonight. I would tell him that if he saw Aunt Grace, he should fly to her.

April 5, 2011

After today's visit Cheryl told us that she thought Scott's death was imminent and that if anyone needed to come to say goodbye, now was the time. We called Kim, she came home and our entire family came to say goodbye. Everyone went in one by one to spend a few special moments with Scott and share how special he had been to us. It was so painful, but Scott tried to ease everyone. When his cousin Mike came to say goodbye, he stood at Scott's bed, unable to say the words. It was quiet, then Scott spoke. "Mike, I want you to know that you are the funniest of all of us and I love you." Mike seemed relieved and said he loved him too. I remember walking out of the room, holding back tears and clutching my heart. As soon as I saw Eileen and Barbara I burst out crying, telling them about their conversation. Even then, Scott made it okay for others and I could not have been more proud of him.

I will never forget this day. A few days before, Cheryl had told us that these were Scott's final days. Kim's job gave her a leave of absence so she could be home with us and two of Scott's cousins were in from their out of state colleges. I woke that morning and wanted to go for a walk since family was arriving that afternoon. As I was walking, I remembered that it was Grace's birthday. Scott and Aunt Grace had such a special bond. He adored her and she truly got a kick out of him, always delighting in his laughter and mischievous antics. As Scott grew up and Grace got older, he took it upon himself to visit her, riding his bike to the nearest convenience store for a box of cookies. Together they would snack, talk and watch TV. She would joke that they always ended up watching his favorite cartoons. When Grace passed away seven years earlier, Scott was so sad but happy that he had special memories with her.

I began to talk to Grace. "Grace, I know it's your birthday today, but please, take him with you. Please, no more pain. He is ready to go. Please, no more pain."

Then I continued on my walk and asked God to give me strength for the day. Soon after I returned home, family members began to arrive. Gene's sister Barbara brought a large box of amazing looking cupcakes. Everyone gathered in the living room except Scott, who was in his room. I went to his room and asked him if he wanted to come into the living room. He did, so we put him on the swivel chair, then wheeled him in and placed him on the couch with the oxygen machine next to him. I showed him the cupcakes.

"Don't these look so delicious?" I said. He nodded.

"Shouldn't we ask Aunt Grace? She's in my room," Scott said.

Everyone's jaw dropped.

"Oh wait, isn't she dead?" he said.

We nodded; our mouths still open.

A little while later, Scott asked to go back to his bed. He wanted to sleep. After he was settled in, I returned to the living room. We began talking about what Scott had said. I then told them about my walk and what I had said to Grace. I know Grace heard me, I think she came to see him and decided it was not his time yet. But I know that they are now in communication and that gives me comfort.

During the next couple of weeks, Scott deteriorated. Kim would read to him, he really enjoyed that. We would listen to the Beatles, watch TV and just talk. He would tell us how he wanted us to live without him, how I could only be sad for three days. I think I mourned my pet gerbil for more than three days, but I promised him that I would try every day. He told us how much he loved us and how he loved our life together.

Soon, he stopped talking and was rarely awake. He was sweating profusely. I would wash him with a cool washcloth many times a day. Sometimes as I washed him, I would tell him that he needed to "fly" now. I would tell him to fly to Heaven and I was so happy that he was mine. This is something that I would say to Kim and Scott when they were growing up, mostly when I was saying good night. *I'm so happy you're mine.*

April 26, 2011

Scott was very agitated. He was sweating a great deal and although he was unable to speak, he made it known through his eyes that he wanted to leave his bed. Around 10:00 p.m., we washed him with cool water, changed his clothes, and placed him in bed with me. His breathing was very rapid and he was uncomfortable. I called hospice. The nurse told me to give him another dose of medication, so I did. He was on my side of the bed with the oxygen machine on the floor next to him. Lucy was also on the floor next to him. I was on Gene's side. Gene was on the couch, Kim was upstairs in her room. I snuggled close to him and told him again how much he was loved. I prayed that he would fly that night. I then fell asleep to the rhythm of the oxygen machine.

Gene woke me around 5:00 a.m. It was April 27, 2011.

"Chris, he's not breathing," he said.

I leaned over and put my head on his chest. I did not hear a heartbeat. The oxygen machine was still. I removed the tube from his nose and kissed his cheek. He was still warm. I kissed him all over his face, while I'm saying goodbye, while I'm telling him I love him. I asked Gene to get Kim. He went upstairs. I continued to kiss Scott goodbye. Then it hit me, the saying parents hear as soon as they become parents. "Your children are a gift from God." I must have heard this saying a hundred times. During those tough teenage years, I even wanted to return that gift, I thought jokingly. But, suddenly, this is what made sense. After kissing Scott for about the 20th time, I looked up to God.

"Thank you," I said. "Thank you for giving him to me for 22 years. He was a gift, but now he has to go Home to you. You knew he was going to get sick and die. You trusted me to love him, care for him and prepare him to go back to you."

Kim and Gene came downstairs and said their goodbyes. Although we knew this day was coming and we were glad that his pain was over, it was still so overwhelmingly sad.

Then the phone calls began. First, hospice had to come and pronounce him. Scott wanted to donate his eyes, so that needed to happen and hospice would help with that as well. Then the funeral home was called. We stayed with Scott until they arrived. Then family, friends and our church were called. Our hearts were broken, but arrangements had to be made.

It was decided that a wake would be held at the funeral home on April 29th and a memorial would be held at our church on April 30. Scott's childhood pastor, who was also the father of two of Scott's friends, joined our current minister for the memorial service. The funeral home was filled with pictures of Scott and flowers, but was most especially filled with people who loved Scott and for whose lives he made such a difference. Scott told me to give out his graduation picture and on the back, put his favorite Beatles quote, "And in the end the love you take is equal to the love you make."

The eulogy at the memorial was beautiful and as Scott requested, "Let It Be" by The Beatles played to a clip of his first solo skydive. Although we had intended to keep the service simple with eulogies from cousins Mike and Gene, Scott's friends asked to say some special words for their friend. They did and added a very special voice to the service. It was amazing, a wonderful tribute to his amazing life. Our church provided space and cooked for the many guests after the service, a gesture that still humbles me.

Now came the hard part—how to live life without my son. This seemed impossible.

Do you know what grief feels like? It's like a thousand pounds pressing on your shoulders and every inch of you, from the top of your head to your toes, is throbbing in pain. You don't think this feeling will ever go away.

Gene

As March turned to April of 2011, there was no doubt that we were in the final stages. Our son was dying and it would happen soon. He was seldom getting out of bed; the oxygen tank was his constant companion and he was sleeping most of the time. Cheryl, the hospice nurse visited every day and we sat with Scott for hours on end, sometimes praying, other times reading to him, but mostly just cherishing the little time that was left.

A month or so earlier, Scott and I were sitting in his room watching the Knicks, a pastime we had come to share. He seemed okay when we started watching the game. At a break I turned to say something and saw that he was crying, which he seldom did in front of me. He usually saved such emotions for his mom. When I asked him about it, he said "Dad I am 22 years old and I am dying!" He wasn't angry, it was like he still couldn't believe that all this was happening or maybe he knew it was happening soon. I asked if he wanted his mom. "No," he said, "I want you to give me a hug." Surprised, but also glad he wanted me this time, I climbed into bed with him, and as we embraced with all the strength he could muster, he poked his finger into my chest and said, "What you did to mom, Kim and I was fucked up." I told him, "I know it was and I am sorry." In that moment I knew he had forgiven me. I had tried to make amends before, on several occasions, but he wasn't ready to hear me. Thankfully, that evening he was and he did on his terms. I felt we were at peace, father and son.

It was mostly just the four of us, Scott, Kim, Chris and I in his final week or so. Kim would read to him; Chris and I would just sit by his side. At times we would all be in his room reminiscing. Scott was so weak he could barely speak, but I felt he was able to share our nostalgia. As the latter days of April rolled by, we knew Scott's time was near. Every morning after a fitful sleep I would go across the hall and check on him, always fearful of what I might find. On the night of April 26, I carried him into our bed to be with his mom and went out to the couch. I probably went in to check on him three or four times, only to see his frail form hanging on, his breathing so shallow and slight. I checked on my son one last time at about 5:00 am on the morning of April 27th 2011, to find that his life, as we knew it to be, had finally left his body.

Chris was asleep and I stared at them both for a few moments. One of them was gone and his mother's life would never be the same. I gently shook Chris' shoulder and when she was awake enough to understand, I told her that our beautiful son was gone. Or was he?

PART III - After
I Got Your Back, Mom

For the past eight years there have been many signs from Scott showing me that he's okay and that he does watch over me. I noticed that when I was in the most pain, there would be a sign—immediately. At first, I thought that I might be going a little crazy, but I soon felt comforted and began to realize that something greater was happening. I felt thrilled at the connection and a deep inner peace permeated my core and gave me strength to move through the process of grieving. I believe that, in Heaven, God gives everyone a job to do. I believe Scott's job was to help teach people that there is a Heaven, that our loved ones are still with us, just not physically. I envisioned him at the Newcomer's Meeting in Heaven volunteering me (as he loved to do) to be the recipient of his messages. This is really God's story and Scott's story, I am just the messenger.

A few days after the memorial, I finally made my way out to the front porch. It was a beautiful, warm day in early May. Just weeks before, I had brought my houseplants outside to soak up the sun after a long winter. Now I wanted to point my face to the sun and just breathe. I was exhausted. Of course, Lucy was by my side. She hadn't left my side since Scott died –and refused to go into Scott's room although she had been there throughout his illness. She was also grieving, sometimes I heard her moaning. As we were sitting there, a wave of cold air came over me. It was so cold that I shivered. I was taken aback because the temperature that day was about 80 degrees.

As I felt the cold pass over me, I said out loud, "Scott, is that you, are you okay?"

The cold lingered for a few seconds, then disappeared. I didn't tell anyone about this experience. I was afraid people might think that I was having a nervous breakdown. I knew I wasn't having a breakdown, I knew it was my son.

A few weeks after Scott died I was again on the front porch with Lucy. I looked next to me and saw a bird's nest in one of the houseplants. Every Spring for twenty-five years, I have always brought my houseplants outside, but this was the very first time a nest had appeared, I was feeling a little excited –probably the first time I had been excited about anything in the last several months. In the following days, the mother robin sat on her four eggs. She continued to sit there even with Lucy and I on the porch. The bird and I had an unspoken agreement, you don't bother me, I won't bother you, let's just sit here and breathe. So we did. I sat there and watched her sit on her eggs. I watched as three beaks peeked up at her. I watched her feed them and teach them to fly. I then watched as they all flew away. When they were gone, I looked in the nest, one blue egg remained. I put that egg in the garden. That night, Scott's nurse Cheryl came for dinner. I told her all about the bird's nest.

"There were four eggs but only three hatched?" Cheryl asked.

I nodded.

"That's the way it is. There were four of you, now there are three."

I immediately got the connection.

Upon closer inspection, I noticed a blue thread running through the nest, which you could say is God. Or you could say it is Scott. Or you could say it is Hope. I believe that it is all three. So I have God, Scott and Hope. Somehow, I knew that I would be all right.

At the beginning of June, I was feeling strong enough to resume my walks. On another beautiful day, I headed to a route more isolated than usual. As I was walking, I began to pray. I started my prayer by saying thank you to God for all he has given me, a wonderful husband, an amazing daughter and family and friends who love me. I was so grateful that I was Scott's mom. He taught me so much, especially how to live fully and love deeply and I am a better person because I was his mom.

After I prayed, I then talked to Scott. I told him all that was going on that day. I told him that I loved him and missed him every minute. I then told him that I was going to have a good day and that I hoped he was doing something fun. I said goodbye and blew him a kiss. I have been doing this every day since.

July 4, 2011

Scott had been gone about 10 weeks by the Fourth of July—yet another holiday to endure. Memorial Day passed in a blur and now the Fourth of July. Before Scott passed, I never really noticed how many holidays there were. I invited my parents and Eileen over for a barbecue and after dinner, we all went to see fireworks. The plan was to keep busy, in hopes of preventing me from crying. It seemed that when I was quiet and still, the tears came. The crowd began to fill the area and I noticed all the families. I saw the young children excited and people enjoying themselves. I began to feel a panic attack coming and I tried to calm myself.

As the fireworks started, I began talking to Scott in my head.

I miss you, buddy. You loved fireworks. Are you watching these?

I looked up at the start of the show and in the middle of the sky was the letter *S*. I pointed it out. Everyone looked up to see another letter *S*.

Soon, you could hear the crowd saying, "Look at the letter *S*."

It was so cool. I went to sleep that night convinced that Scott was watching over me and I thanked him for that.

While Gene and I were out running errands, we began to notice all the Christmas decorations. I started to cry and couldn't stop. I missed my son. We left the store and decided to get some lunch. As we headed toward the pizza parlor, we noticed a woman who resembled Grace. We smiled at this and remembered when Scott saw Grace in his room. We talked about what a special relationship they had. Nearing the restaurant, we came upon a big, gaudy white SUV that was parked right in front. You couldn't miss it. The license plate read, *GRACE 4 SM*. Grace for Scott McMurray? I laughed.

"Gene, do you know what this means? They are in cahoots together in Heaven!"

Another sign that my boy was watching over me, that he was okay. I knew something really powerful was happening.

All of Scott's friends joined forces in recognition of Scott's upcoming birthday and planned a St. Baldrick's fund raiser at a local bar. Many of our family, friends, and Scott's friends celebrated his life and memory that night in hoisting a few and more than one left the bar that night with much less hair than they arrived with. Several thousand dollars were raised that night for pediatric cancer research in Scott's name. This event continued for the next several years through Scott's twenty-fifth birthday in 2013.

November 15, 2011

It was my birthday, my fiftieth and I was driving to the dentist in tears. Everyone talks about their fiftieth birthday and how they will celebrate. Some people have big parties. Some people go on trips. I used to dream about what I would do. I wanted to take a family vacation to Disney World—to just have a blast, just the four of us. Then Scott got sick and everything changed. I didn't care about a trip or a fancy dinner. I just wanted my family together, my whole family—the four of us. And I would never have that again. Never. So, my crying was getting worse. I was probably banging on the steering wheel as well. The sun was glaring through the windshield, so I pulled down the visor. As I did, a large manila envelope knocked me on the head. I put it on the seat next to me. When I arrived at the dentist, I opened the envelope. Inside was an 8x10 picture of Scott and his friends taken at their senior prom. One of Scott's friends had given the picture to Gene and he placed it in the car. I didn't even know about this. I smiled. The picture was beautiful and I believe Scott knocked me on the head to wish me a happy birthday. He would definitely do this.

It was our first Thanksgiving without Scott. The night before, I had a very rough night and when I woke up that morning, my head hurt and my face was swollen from crying. It was Thanksgiving and I didn't know if I could do it. How could I sit around a table and give thanks? Everyone would be there— everyone except Scott. I didn't want to sit at a table, I really wanted to stay in bed. Kim was home, so that was not an option. I had to get up for her. But, before the Thanksgiving festivities, I would take my walk. I quickly dressed, putting a large hat over my head, wore a bulky coat and even put on sunglasses. I didn't want to take the chance of someone stopping to talk to me and this outfit was clearly saying, "stay away". Then, I began my walk and started to pray.

"Please, God, please give me strength for today. This is so hard. How am I supposed to be thankful today? For what? I don't feel gratitude, all I feel is anger. Everyone is at their table with their families, but my son is not here. It's Thanksgiving, but the last thing I feel is gratitude." As I was walking, soon my body and mind calmed and I realized something. A few weeks after Scott passed I received a letter from the eye bank and was told that because of Scott's cornea donation, the eyesight of two men had been restored. I started to think about that. At two separate Thanksgiving tables this year, two men were clearly seeing their families and their beautiful dinner - what a gift! Quite possibly during their dinner blessing they might remember Scott. I felt proud, proud that my son made such a selfless decision, even as he was facing death, he helped others. I returned home from my walk feeling better, I wasn't thankful, but I was proud. I decided that for today, that was enough.

Then I talked to Scott. Told him how proud I was of him, so happy he was mine. Then I asked him for help.

"I don't want to do this without you. I can't be at this table without you, please help me," I cried.

A little while later, we arrived at Eileen's home. The table was beautiful and she had two honeysuckle candles in the middle to honor Scott. Honeysuckle was his favorite scent and we always had them burning when he was sick.

We all gathered at the table and held hands. Gene began the blessing. As he spoke, he began to cry. We were still holding hands and looking down when, all of a sudden, one of the candles fell. It was not a gentle fall, like a loose candle, but like someone had intentionally knocked it down. We all stared at the fallen candle, looked at each other and laughed.

"That's right, Scott, tell Dad to stop crying! That's so annoying!"

We all knew that we had just seen something pretty amazing. The rest of the night we told Scott stories and watched YouTube videos that he would have liked. That night as I closed my eyes, I told Scott, *Thank you, that was so cool.* I also thanked God for giving me the strength that I so very much needed. As I was drifting off to sleep, I thought it was a good day.

November 29, 2011

It was Scott's birthday. On this day twenty-three years
earlier, I gave birth to a beautiful baby boy. November was killing
me—too many special days. We struggled to find a way to
commemorate Scott's birthday and settled on organizing a pizza
party for the oncology unit at Children's Hospital in honor of
Scott, a tradition we still continue.

That afternoon, I was asked to babysit for the neighbor's
two children I had been babysitting for the past four years,
whenever my schedule would allow. At first, I hesitated about
taking the job on this particular day, thinking it might be too
difficult, but decided it could be a good distraction. I did not tell
the parents that it was Scott's birthday, I just wanted to get through
the day.

When I arrived, the children—Evan, 4, and Katie, 2—asked
if we could play with Play-Doh. No problem, I set everything up to
make a farm with the Play-Doh. Katie was happy with this, but
Evan was not.

"Let's make a birthday cake!" he shouted.

"No, we're making a farm," I said, a little stunned.

*There will be no birthday cake today. In fact, this day will
never have a birthday cake again*, I thought to myself.

Soon, Evan joined in on making the farm, after which I
cooked dinner for them. They were very well-behaved, they used
their manners and ate everything, so I said they could pick a
dessert. Evan's eyes lit up.

"I know, a birthday party with ice cream!"

Again with this birthday party, I thought. Before I could answer, he opened the freezer and started getting out the ice cream. In his excitement, he added the chocolate syrup and sprinkles. We were having a party despite my efforts to the contrary! We put the ice cream and toppings in our bowls and sat down at the table. As we were eating, I explained to them that I was sad because it was Scott's birthday and I missed him.

"Because he died?" Evan asked in a way that only a four-year-old could.

I nodded my head.

"Well, Happy Birthday, Scott," he said, looking up.

"Happy Birthday, Scott," Katie and I said, looking up.

We smiled. We were having an ice cream birthday party! When the children's mother returned, I told her what had happened.

"Did you know it was Scott's birthday?" she asked Evan.

Evan shook his head no.

As I was walking home and thinking about this day, I started laughing.

"I am having more contact with you now than I did your first semester of college!" I said, looking up.

Did Scott nudge Evan into having a birthday party? I like to think so.

December 2011

This was our first Christmas without Scott. I was prepared for this—or so I thought. A couple of months prior, I began dreading Christmas, I knew that I had to get away, far away. I went on the computer and before I knew it, I had booked a turtle conservation trip for the three of us. Gene was in the living room watching a ball game and I was booking us to save the turtles! The thing about the computer is once you press send, you're done! Now I had to tell Gene. I tried to make it sound very exciting—a trick I learned from being a day care provider for twenty years.

"Guess what we're doing for Christmas?" I said.

"What?" Gene replied.

"We're saving the turtles!" I shouted.

His reaction was less than enthusiastic. In fact, he was pretty nervous, and I think he was questioning my sanity. Kim, on the other hand, was excited about this trip. One out of two wasn't bad!

We arrived in Costa Rica on the nineteenth, Kim's 25th birthday. We worked with the turtles until the twenty-fourth. Our job was to walk the beach at night when hundreds of sea turtles would come on shore, so we could observe them and document them digging their nests and laying their eggs. We would measure and also tag them. It ended up being filled with fun, with many adventures and laughs.

On Christmas Eve we were in a cab, driving to a hotel. We were looking forward to a few days in a hotel with real showers since we smelled like turtles. It was quiet in the cab. The driver did not speak English and the music playing was Spanish. I was thinking about how much Scott would have loved this trip. Then the music changed. 'Hey Jude' from The Beatles began to play. The three of us looked at each other knowingly. Tears welled in my eyes and Kim grabbed my hand. We play this song a lot. The line "Take a sad song and make it better" was one Scott had relied on when he was sick and has become somewhat of a family anthem. Even now, it is something we say when we are volunteering with hospice families. We even have cards with these lyrics, along with a drawing of Scott skydiving. "Take a sad song and make it better." Everyone should do this. When we arrived at the hotel, I had a good cry—partly from exhaustion, mostly because I missed my son. When I closed my eyes that Christmas Eve, I pictured Scott in Heaven being a part of the biggest birthday party. Merry Christmas, Scott.

I was out running errands for a couple of hours. When I returned, Gene told me this story. He was outside on the porch thinking about Scott. It was still and quiet. Gene asked Scott to ring the chimes if he was there. The chimes rang.

A little while later, Gene was upstairs in his office working. There was an upcoming drawing at his office for various monetary amounts, from $100 to $1,000. Gene asked Scott to pull his name and he won $700! I admit, my first thought was to have Scott win the lottery for us, but right then and there, we decided that we would *never* again ask for money.

It had been one year since Scott passed. Kim came home so that we could all be together. We decided to see a movie (one that Scott would have liked) and go to dinner. This was always a fun thing for our family to do, so that was how we would honor his anniversary. After waking up, I decided to go for a walk. As usual, I prayed. I thanked God for all that He had given me. I told God that I understood that He needed Scott and I did have comfort in knowing that Scott was with him, but I just really missed my son.

Then I talked to Scott. As I did so, I found myself telling him how grateful I was for all the signs he had shown me—all to show me that he was okay. I told him that I missed him, but I reminded myself that the person who I was grieving was the one who had held me up this entire year. I meant this. Every time that I had cried out for him, he answered with a sign.

I realized that he was called Home because he had a job to do. I promised him that I would be okay and that I would try every day, but I also reminded him that he couldn't always watch over me. He needed to do his job. I then blew him a kiss goodbye, again.

May 2012

It was Memorial Day weekend and we rented a condo in Mt. Pleasant, South Carolina. Our family friends, the Carnaghis, agreed to take care of Lucy for us. Gene and I had been talking about moving out of New York and South Carolina appealed to us. During our two week stay, we went house hunting and put in an offer on a two bedroom condo. We decided that, for a few years, we could live in New York and South Carolina until we felt ready to make the 'big move'.

On my walk that morning, I received a phone call from Cyndi Carnaghi, our friend and neighbor who was dog sitting with Lucy while we were gone. She was worried. It seemed as though something was wrong with Lucy. I told her to just make sure she was comfortable and to call me in a couple of hours with an update. As I was walking, I asked Scott to watch over Lucy, remembering their special bond whenever Scott came home. I could hear him coming up the cement steps, his sneakers squeaking. As soon as he would reach the wooden stairs, he would yell out, "Lucy, Lucy!" She would hear this and run to the door, always there when he walked in. I smile when I think of this.

That afternoon as we were signing the contracts for the condo, Gene's cell phone rang. We let it go to voice mail. After the meeting, we saw that it was Gary Carnaghi, Cyndi's dad, who had called. Lucy had passed away. We were devastated, but we also felt bad for Gary, Diana, Cyndi, and Matt Carnaghi, who were there to see it.

Now, Lucy needed to be cremated per Scott's request. You know you have good friends when they offer to take your pet to the vet for cremation, and they did. Her remains were to be mixed with Scott's and they would be going to Yosemite. When I returned to New York, Matt came to see me. He gave me a picture taken of Lucy a couple of days before she died. She was in the backyard, looking happy. On the top left of the image is a bright light beaming on Lucy. I like to think that was Scott.

A few days later, we took the Carnaghi family to dinner at one of the local pubs. There was a DJ, so we requested The Beatles "Lucy in the Sky with Diamonds." We changed the lyrics to "Lucy in the Sky with Scotty," and we sang them loudly. It was a good night. They are together.

I was offered a part-time assistant teacher position at the nursery school at our church, where I would be working with two-year-old's, three times a week. I felt ready to work part-time.

As I pulled into the parking lot on my first day of work, I began to feel nervous. What if seeing those cute little children reminded me too much of who I was missing? Maybe this was a mistake. I sat in the car and had a mild panic attack. I prayed for strength and talked to Scott.

"Will this be all right?" I asked.

Finally, I walked into the classroom and soon the children arrived. One little girl was wearing a Beatles T-shirt. I smiled, thinking that I was going to be just fine.

One day while babysitting Evan and Katie, I decided to take them to the park. I was sitting on a bench watching them play when I suddenly became emotional. Watching the children with their mothers laughing and playing, reminded me of days past with Kim and Scott. I wiped away my tears and tried to concentrate on Evan and Katie. Not happening.

"I just miss you," I whispered. "Do you miss me?"

All of a sudden, a boy wearing a Superman shirt ran up to me, looked at me for a brief moment, then ran off to play. I smiled at him. Then another boy, wearing a Beatles shirt stood in front of me. I smiled again. Superman and the Beatles! Scott's favorite things!

"You do miss me!"

I had gone to bed at my usual time, around 10:00 p.m. Suddenly, I bolted up from bed. I looked at the clock, it was 3:15 a.m. I woke Gene up.

"I'm not dreaming," I said. "I just went to Heaven with Scott!"

I then described every detail. I told him that first I parked my car in Yonkers. (I don't know why it was Yonkers, I very rarely go there.) I was very concerned about leaving my car there. Scott and a boy with curly dark hair approached me, I was so happy to see him. He came closer and put his arm around my shoulders, and I remember it felt so good.

"How are you doing, Mom?" he said in my ear.

I just hugged him.

"Want to see something really cool?" he asked.

The next thing I knew we were standing on a highway with cars whizzing by us. Scott ran from one side to another, right through the cars. I got really nervous. He did this two more times, then came to me.

"That is dangerous," I said. "You could hurt yourself or someone else."

He started to walk away.

"Mrs. McMurray, Scott can't hurt anyone or himself because he died," said the boy with the curly hair.

I got mad at this and told him not to say that. Now they were both walking away.

"Come back," I called. "You're right. You're right! Scott did die."

They both returned to me.

"Come with me," Scott said. He put his arm around me again. "It'll be fun," he whispered. "I got your back."

Somehow, we ended up in what seemed like a frat house. I smelled liquor and people were smoking and laughing, everyone was having a good time. Shots of a red drink were going around.

"No, thanks. I have to get my car, it's in Yonkers," I said. People laughed.

"Mrs. McMurray, tonight you don't have to worry about your car," one of them said.

I looked around. There was a long picnic table with all kinds of people sitting there, laughing. I sat down. An African American woman with bright red lipstick and the most beautiful smile sat across from me. I looked for Scott. He had ditched me, but I was fine. I asked the people at the table if I was in Heaven. They nodded and laughed. I asked about my car again; if it would be all right in Yonkers. They said it would be fine. I then did a couple of shots. I was feeling woozy but happy. I said if this is Heaven, then I want to see my friend Lori's two brothers, Kenny and Paul. Both passed away young, had been gone about ten years. I felt a tap on my shoulder and when I turned around, it was Paul. I was so excited as I hugged him. I told him how handsome he looked. He told me how funny it was that Kurt (Lori, Kenny and Paul's nephew) was giving their brother John a run for his money! We laughed because John was always causing trouble as a child.

A girl sitting next to me was wearing a wedding dress. She told me that she died on her honeymoon in a skiing accident.

"That's really rough," I said.

When I turned to my left, there was Kenny. I smiled, I was so happy. He gave me a look that said, "Calm down, don't embarrass me."

"Come on, this is so cool," I whispered to him. He nodded and smiled, then I woke up.

Was this a dream? Was this a visitation? I remember everything about it—the smells, the taste, every detail. I never remember my dreams.

It would be like Scott to run through cars on a highway. It would be like him to ditch me at a party. Maybe a part of Heaven is like a big frat party. At the long picnic table, everyone seemed happy. Doesn't that sound like Heaven? One thing does bother me, though. I am mad that I was worried about my car. Even in Heaven, I am too responsible.

It was Memorial Day weekend and we were at Yosemite to spread Scott and Lucy's ashes. The three of us were there, along with Barbara, Eileen, and Scott's cousins. My friend Lori and her family also joined us.

We did not jump from Half Dome, but we found a perfect spot at its foot where there was a beautiful meadow surrounding Mirror Lake. Each person had a private moment to walk around and reflect while spreading some of the ashes. We cried, we smiled and we hugged. Afterward, we all went for a walk. Upon returning to the campsite, I just cried—hard. I guess this was another goodbye, but I did find comfort in knowing that we had fulfilled all of Scott's wishes. What an amazing thing.

I was asked to be the assistant teacher for the four-year-old class that year. I felt ready to do this and was happy with the placement. The day before school was to begin, I went in to help set up the classroom. As I was working, the director came in and sat next to me. She started telling me about the class. She told me who the quiet kids were, who the not-so-quiet kids were and who might need some extra help. She was sure that I was going to love this class. Then she told me about a little girl who was undergoing cancer treatment. This was the first time a student was attending this school while in treatment. I was speechless. Why hadn't she told me this before? I was not happy. I was scared that I couldn't handle it and I was due to start the next day!

When I got home, I told Gene. He shared his concerns. He was worried that this might be too hard for me emotionally, that I was doing better and this might set me back. I called Kim, she had the same reaction as Gene. But I was supposed to start the next day! I had a plan. After the meet and greet, I would speak to the director and discuss whether or not I was the right person for this job, at this time.

The next morning the parents and children arrived at school. I saw their smiling faces as they entered the classroom. Then I saw her, a little bald girl heading straight to the dress-up area to put on a princess dress. Her mother was behind her, looking terrified as if she were about to cry. There went my talk with the director. I approached the mom and asked to speak with her in the hallway. I introduced myself and explained that I knew exactly what her family was going through and promised to take good care of her precious little girl. I asked her to bring me her chemo schedule as well as a digital thermometer. The mom burst out crying, then hugged me.

"I've been so worried," she said.

I asked her daughter's name.

"Abby," she said.

Abby was the name of one of Scott's closest friends. She was in my day care as a child and they remained buddies. Abby just completed medical school, is currently in residency, her career choice largely influenced after standing by Scott during his illness and his death.

As I was walking home from school, I started talking to Scott. "I know you had something to do with this. I promise you she will have fun." I had a wonderful experience that year in nursery school. I worked well with the teacher and I felt that I was very helpful to Abby. My experience with Scott made me aware of some of the risky side effects of chemo. For example, a few days after Abby received chemo, I would place my hand on the back of her neck or face several times a day. Looking at me you would think that I was showing affection but I was making sure she was not feverish. Fevers could be symptomatic of sepsis which required immediate medical attention. I also took extra care of Abby during gymnastics time or any other physical play. I would notice shortness of breath and I would ask her if she wanted to come and sit on my lap. Another symptom Abby showed was that she sometimes walked on her toes. One time a teacher corrected her and I explained that chemo causes tenderness in the soles of the feet. I remember Scott complaining of this and he would sometimes tip toe. Giving him foot massages did help, although not completely.

Abby had a wonderful school year and when she walked across the stage at Nursery School Graduation, I was so proud, clapping through tears of joy, I looked at her parents and they were crying and clapping too!

I was talking with an acquaintance when she mentioned the recent passing of her mother-in-law. She was deeply saddened saying she could not accept it. She then asked me if I had accepted Scott's death. I was at a loss for words. I had actually never thought of this. Accept his death? What does that mean? In my head, I knew the facts. Scott had died. I knew this, but if I stopped and truly thought about it, I would crumble. I think I separated my head from my heart. My head accepted and understood that Scott had technically died, but my heart did not feel this. Does 'accepting' his death mean that I am happy with 'the Plan?' I don't think so. In the years since, I have never thought of this. I knew this was God's Plan but was it a Plan for me? For Scott? I'm not supposed to question God's Plan, but I do. I also know not to ask why. Sometimes there are no answers.

On the anniversary of the date that we learned Scott's cancer had returned, Gene was in South Carolina and I was very sad. I'd been feeling down all week, even my shoulders felt heavy. I was able to go to work, but other than that, I usually stayed in the house and ate huge amounts of melted cheese, my favorite comfort food.

That night, an old friend called to ask if I wanted to go for a walk. I agreed, thinking it might help. I suggested the more isolated route, but she wanted the flatter route to ease her knee, so we decided on the route that I usually walked with Gene. During our walk, she talked about her son and his struggles. I listened. Then I told her this was a rough week for me because I was missing my son. We remarked how easy our daughters were.

"We had to have the boy!" she quipped.

I laughed and looked to the sky. When I lowered my head, there in the cement was the name *Scott*. I stopped.

"Do you see this?" I asked. "This is his handwriting and look, there are his footprints."

Sure enough, there were footprints in the cement leaving the scene of the crime. I put my foot over his prints. Based on the size, he must have been in middle school. He wasn't even allowed down here in the middle of White Plains!

This was a route that Gene and I had walked a hundred times before and I am just seeing it now?

As soon as I got home, I called Gene and told him. The next day, I brought Eileen to the cement. She noticed something else. Underneath the word *Scott* was an *M*. I had no doubt this was my son.

Before I went to sleep that night, I told Scott how amazing it was to see the footprints and his name. It was just what I needed and I thanked him again for watching over me.

A month prior, Gene and I put the house up for sale. We were ready to move to South Carolina full-time and we were ready for a fresh start.

The house had been in the family for 60 years and we were so grateful for all of the wonderful memories.

On my walks, I would pray for the house. "Dear God, I just want a good family in this house; this home is so special."

It was so important for us to find the right owners, that before we put it on the market, we invited families who we knew were renting, offering it to them first. Unfortunately, it was very hard for those families to save for a down payment when they had small children, so we listed the house with a real estate agent.

After five weeks, we got an offer. It was a little too low, so we countered. We went back and forth a little bit and finally, they signed the contract.

At the end of July, we officially moved to South Carolina. I am so happy to say that the house went to a very lovely family. The new owner's name? Scott!

October 2016

Even now, years later, Scott still makes his presence known. During the time that Hurricane Matthew was impacting Charleston, I had the following exchange via text with the wife of the pastor from our church in New York:

Hi, Chris. So nice to chat with you last night. Wanted to share something. Today at gymnastics a woman who helped me teach Sunday School last week and I were chatting. She is fairly new to the church so I do not know her well. Anyhow, pre-kids she was a nurse practitioner in pediatric oncology at Montefiore. You guessed it, she knew Scott. She said when they were getting assignments for the day, everybody wanted Scott. She said he was an incredible person. Kind to all he met, friendly, warm, encouraging to others, with a good sense of humor. His parents were amazing too. With all they were going through, they were a ray of hope and encouragement to everyone. There aren't many McMurrays around. COINCIDENCE? I THINK NOT. What are the chances!!!! I agree, there are too few McMurrays around. Who would think that in our church in Summit there would be a woman connected to you? That book will be written and published. God knew you needed a pick me up and once again, He provided.

Hi, Donna. Thanks for checking on us. We're staying at a friend's house, made of bricks, safe. Gene just walked to our home—no electric, but thankfully no flooding or broken roof. Grateful! Pretty cool thing, right after the rain stopped, Gene called me into our friend's TV room. He pointed out the window to a makeshift pond on the golf course and there was a boy, about 15 years old, who looked just like Scott – same build, hair, and skimboarding into the pond just like Scott would do. He took a break, texted his friends and soon, there they were, all having a blast. I said, "It's Scott." I know it was him, thinking of us, helping us through our first Carolina hurricane.

Donna continued, *Amazing how Scott continues to give you peace during storms (literally or figuratively) or during frightening times. Well, you always raised him to care for others.*

Anniversaries are always a particularly tough time, seven years later it is still tough. This year Gene and I were walking on the beach and of course talking about Scott. I talked about how much I missed him and my hope that he is proud of me. As we walked a little further, something in the surf caught my eye. A makeshift heart was etched in the sand along with the words "I miss you." Scott, again!!

June 2018

It is now June 12, 2018. Gene and I are driving home from an appliance store when the subject of Scott's age came up. Gene calculated and remarked that Scott would be turning 30 next November. I couldn't believe this. "No," I said, that can't be right, 30?" I soon realized Gene was right. Kim would be 32 in December, so yes, Scott would be 30. I then began to tremble and cry. "What would he be like?" I cried. "Would he have made a difference in people's lives? Would he have made the world a better place?" So many unanswered questions. Because Barbara is visiting us, Gene aimlessly drives in various neighborhoods to give me a chance to calm down before heading home. When I arrive, I busy myself with gardening and Barbara has no idea of my pain.

Three days later I receive this text from a girl a few years younger than Scott who also grew up attending Hitchcock Presbyterian Church. I was her mentor for confirmation when she was in the 9th grade and we occasionally keep in touch.

"Hey, been thinking of you. Last night my neighbor and some friends were hanging out and we got into a discussion of who we knew from high school. They all went to White Plains. Scott came up and for a good hour or two I heard a bunch of beautiful stories about him in high school. One that really stuck out was that in 8th or 9th grade one of them had a class with Scott and a kid that tended to be left out because he had a disability. They talked about how they watched Scott befriend the kid and will never forget when Scott brought him a birthday cake and presents on his birthday and how Scott took it upon himself to make sure he wasn't excluded. My heart was so warm hearing all of these amazing stories about him. I thought that you'd appreciate knowing that people still talk about how amazing Scott was, that he's remembered so wonderfully."

My response, "Jenn, I cannot thank you enough for this beautiful message. I miss him every day and to hear a story like this just warms my heart. It is still surreal to me; I still cannot believe that he is not here but hearing how he touched people's lives makes me so proud. Thank you for brightening my day."

After reading Jenn's notes my heart is bursting; I am filled with joy. I did not know of this exchange between Scott and this boy and learning this fills me with pride. This is my son! My questions are answered. He did make a difference in this world, he brought joy, laughter and compassion to others and the world is a better place because of him.

During the Summer of 2018, I started to experience some strange symptoms. At least three times I felt like the room was spinning. I could explain this by rationalizing that I simply had to increase my water intake. After all, it was one hundred degrees and I spend much of my day outside with children. My entire body hurt. I then self-diagnosed arthritis and decided to reduce my exercise regimen. I then noticed it took me longer to do my walk and bicycling was getting harder. I blamed that on my tires needing air. My hands, feet and tongue would sometimes feel like pins and needles, I was also experiencing some memory loss. I was having trouble swallowing and on one occasion, Gene had to resort to the Heimlich maneuver. I was exhausted but attributed that to age and activity – and again, the need for more water.

In the Fall when I attempted to resume my daily walk, I had only gone a short distance before I felt stabbing pains in my feet. So, I came home, took two aspirin and rested. When I went to the bathroom to urinate, my urine was dark brown, the color of Coca Cola. Uh, oh, this is not good. When after four urinations things seemed to return to normal, I took this as a sign that whatever bug I had was clearing up. Except, this continued for the next three days, then it cleared up for two days. I was not dealing with this! After about six days, the discolored urine returned accompanied by chest pains and painful feet. This finally resulted in an emergency room visit. I thought I was having a heart attack. Upon arrival, I was promptly hooked up to an EKG monitor and an IV was inserted. The poking and prodding led to a full scale anxiety attack that brought me back to Scott's ER experiences. "Scott, how did you do this? Help me be brave like you were." Of course, when the doctor's first name was Scott, I immediately felt some relief and no, it wasn't a heart attack, I was discharged from the ER with orders to see a urologist. This was accomplished in short order and after some lab work and consultation, I learned that the brown urine was not the result of blood as had been originally conjectured, but rather muscle decompensation. This led to an immediate referral to a neurologist – that day. After more poking, prodding and sticking my extremities with needles which I didn't feel, the observation was made that I had serious muscle loss – cause unknown. However, some of the suspected explanations were daunting to say the least – a brain tumor, Multiple Sclerosis, ALS, to name a few. An MRI was ordered to narrow down the possibilities but could not be scheduled for two weeks. During that period of relative calm, I took a lesson from Scott and tried to live each day as it came, finding whatever joy I could – I processed these possibilities. A brain tumor or MS, I could manage. ALS not so much. However, during that period of waiting while Gene and I walked, talked and relaxed, I thought that this was a win-win for me. If I had a terminal illness, I would get to be with Scott that much sooner. If not, I would be able to stay with Gene and Kim. I was at peace with whatever the outcome might be.

On the day of the MRI, I babysat a little boy named Ryder and took him to the movies. As we were driving home I noticed my family ring looked different. Looking closer, I saw Scott's topaz birthstone was missing. Pointing this out to Ryder's mom when I brought him home, she noted that this was Scott's way of telling me that he has my back and I will be okay. This thought stayed with me through the MRI and waiting for the results. These results would not be available until after our traditional family Thanksgiving in Washington, DC, which was a new tradition established after Eileen sold her home in White Plains. This in between spot to New York and South Carolina gave us all the opportunity to come together to share the holiday. After a long weekend spent eating, cooking, playing games and sharing time and laughter, I returned home confident that I would be fine. The results of the MRI were negative so none of the feared outcomes were in play. So then, why was I losing muscle? After what seemed almost a casual discussion of the meds I was on, the fact that I took Red Yeast Rice in an effort to control my cholesterol, was mentioned. I was avoiding the traditional statin treatment as there was suspicion it could increase one's risk of Alzheimer's. Since there was a family history, I was cautious in this regard.

In researching the side effects of the Red Rice Yeast, the doctor and I were both startled to see that in rare cases it can cause muscle loss in the urine! We thought we found the culprit and after four weeks off the supplement, my urine was clear, after eight weeks, the tingling in my hands and feet ceased, after twelve weeks, I was feeling much better. Although this whole process was scary, I knew that I would be all right because Scott continued to show me the way.

January 2019

For Christmas, 2018, my good friend Maria gave me a gift of 'a reading' by a Medium. I was excited about this private session and was hoping to hear from Scott. Among other things, I asked him to let me know what to do with this almost completed manuscript, where to send it when the time came. After all, it was Scott's story!

When the session began at Maria's home, after a few moments of quiet, she explained the process. She makes a connection with spirits who have a message and sometimes she can feel their pain, sometimes she can see and hear them directly. It did not take long before she began.

"Your mother, does she have Alzheimer's? I nodded. "Your father is here and he wants you to know that they are connecting and he will be bringing her soon. She has not eaten or drunk in a while and the nurses are using sponges to keep her mouth moist." I nodded again. When she first mentioned my father, my first thought was that I'm in trouble – I usually was with him. She added, "your father thanks you for telling him at his bedside that it was okay to go. Everyone else was telling him to hang on, but you told him it was time to see his parents, his brother, his son and Scott. He said when he let go, the pain stopped and he was free, so "thank you". Again, I nodded. "He also says he's sorry, please forgive him." I asked, "For what?" She explained that my father was acknowledging the hurt, the hole and emptiness in my heart that he and my mother caused. He says that he knew you were being treated unfairly and he didn't do anything to stop it. She continued, "he is showing me your parents with two siblings on one side, you on another. He says that you always did what you wanted, not what they wanted. He also admitted that he secretly admired this, but it created a wedge. He said that you are the strongest person he knows. He said that your mother and sister would never acknowledge the pain they caused you, but he is sorry and his soul is not right. I was not surprised to hear this and satisfied in a way, as I don't think you can hurt those you are supposed to love without suffering consequences. I am happy that he apologized and I do forgive him.

Then she said, "Someone else is stepping forward showing me the number two. Do you have two children?" I nod. "A girl and a boy?" I nod again. She continued, "Wait, this is your son? Your son passed? My neck is hurting," she said. I explained that a sore neck was Scott's first symptom. "He's talking to his grandfather," she continued. "He is telling him that although you caused pain in her heart, she filled me and my sister's soul with so much love. Every day we knew we were loved. She did not repeat the pattern." Tears were filling my eyes. Next she said that Scott wanted to talk about his sister. "He says she is so beautiful and she has long brown hair. He likes when she wears some of his clothes. He also says he protects her because you worry about her." The Medium smiled. "He says that when she is driving he is sitting with her and wants me (the Medium) to say 'Shotgun' loudly." I smiled at the memory. When they were little, they always argued over who got the front seat and 'Shotgun' was the code word. When I got home I called Kim and asked if she had any of Scott's clothes. She does, his pajama bottoms and fraternity shirt.

"Now he wants to talk about his father," the Medium said. "He drinks or used to? Scott is making a drinking motion." I tell her that Gene has been in recovery for a long time. "Does your husband have a chair in your house where he sits, takes off his glasses and meditates?" she asked. I agreed that he meditates but was unsure about the glasses. She continued, "Scott wants his father to know that when he does this, he is connecting with him." When I got home I asked Gene about this. He said that he makes a point to remove his glasses before he begins. He also told me that a week ago he was focusing on Scott and he could feel something different, that he was not alone in the room. Gene was so happy to hear this.

Now the Medium said, "He says you did not send up balloons this year." I was stunned. No, we didn't, although we usually sent balloons up for his birthday, Christmas and his anniversary, but being so close to the ocean I worried about the dolphins and whales. She said Scott is smiling. "That's her heart," he says. She continued, "Did you write a note, putting it in his coffin?" I shook my head no. Looking puzzled, she said that he is writing and hand it to me. I hand it back. This process repeats itself. "What are you writing?" she asked. I tell her about the book and she asks if it's about Scott. I replied that it was being written both about him, and with him. She noted that he was patting himself on the back, saying that he started this. I exclaimed that he did. He also said that I would know where to send it when the time is right. Further specifics were not forthcoming. Before the session ended Scott asked if I have noticed pennies in my path? Jokingly, I suggested that he send twenties! Finally, Scott told the Medium to tell me that we are still a team. She said that he walked over to me kissing my forehead, saying that I am such a great mom. Tears were running down my cheeks as I made my way downstairs to see Maria. Hugging her, I thanked her for such an amazing gift.

When I got home, I reflected on my experience. Before this day I had no plan to attend my mother's funeral when she passes. She was never satisfied with me, was always rejecting, so I had decided not to attend whatever funeral took place. After this experience, however, I resolved to go but to stand strong. I will go for my father who apologized; I will go for my daughter so she will not be alone. I will have to try to forgive my mother at some point and be proud that I did not repeat her patterns. Instead, I loved with my entire heart and soul and I am loved. The next day as I was returning from my walk, I looked down and there was a twenty-dollar bill! I looked up, laughed, thanked Scott, but told him no more money, it's too weird!

I was doing some cleaning and of course I stopped in front of this photo which always makes me smile. Scott was about 20 months old and we were at the Jersey shore with Eileen and her family. Scott loved the beach, he loved the sand, the water and always had so much fun! After being "greased up" with sunscreen, he would roll in the sand and get up with sand in every nook and cranny of his body – when he laughed, you could even see the sand on his teeth!

Scott loved to spread his arms open and tuck his head down so that he would face the ocean backwards. As the waves came to his face, sometimes knocking him down, his giggling was infectious. This little boy was laughing and so were all of the adults watching this delightful scene. It was pure joy, he always brought out the fun and joy in, as well as for others. It still amazes me how transparent these qualities were, even at this young age.

As I was looking at this picture this morning, I saw the number '4' and to the right of that, '11,' the month and year of Scott's death, April, 2011. I excitedly pointed this out to Gene but as he saw it, he did not react the way I hoped, so I called Eileen. She saw it and then noticed more. She observed, "Look, where Scott is raising his arms, doesn't his shadow look like Angel wings? Now, follow the closest wing – that leads to the 4, next to the 4 is an S, next to the S is the 11" - Angel wings, S and Scott's death date. The message here? That God is truly in control, that there is a predetermination and that we are all in this together. The lesson that this reinforced for me is that if we are aware, live in the present and keep our eyes open, the signs are there for us to see. Eileen observed, "We are all just walking each other home." Exactly.

EPILOGUE – Living and Learning
Gene

As I write this, it's been seven years plus since Scott's passing. Our daughter is pursuing a career in Washington, DC; we are a short eight hour car ride away in Charleston. We try to give her some space but are not always successful. Chris and I talk about Scott all the time, mostly reminiscing about his antics or how he made us proud. We obviously still miss him every day. As Chris has detailed in the year or so after his death, we were constantly seeing what we believed were messages from him, some very profound. Those messages now are not so frequent; it's usually in a dream now, when he comes to be with us. I believe that when he first left us he was trying to hang onto this world and his visits were frequent. Eventually his spirit became comfortable on the other side and he is pursuing the possibilities that are there; he has moved on. Don't we all? Maybe that's the lesson in our whole story. A part of us is always dying while another part of us is awakening. Scott has moved from this life to another. I moved from a life of alcohol and drugs to become a responsible and effective part of the ultimate family challenge. Chris and Kim are also transitioning from how it was to how it is. These changes are difficult and painful but are as natural and as necessary as breathing.

So, that's the Story of the McMurray's. We have tried to be as honest as possible, which at times was painful. Some people I am sure would have done things differently or might be perplexed or even at odds with some of the decisions we made. We understand but offer no apologies, we did our best. When you are going through the illness of a loved one, no matter how much help you get and we got plenty, there is a sense of isolation. Every day, upon awakening, we tried to think of Scott first and make the best of a horrible situation. In reality, Scott had the final say on most decisions because he was an adult and most of the time he did the right thing.

This is a family story, Scott was a son, a brother, a nephew and a cousin. We all had the privilege of watching him grow from an irresponsible college freshman to a caring, loving adult in three short years. This was never more evident than our final Christmas together. Scott had four months to live, Chris, Scott, Kim and I had dinner together, then his aunts and cousins arrived to open gifts. Through Scott's lead we had a wonderful, loving Christmas. No fear of dying, no resentments of a life cut short, only the love of family and being together on his favorite holiday. He had come to peace with his destiny and it was up to us to accept it as well. The legacy that Scott left us was best expressed by his beloved Beatles in one of his favorite lines "…and in the end the love you take is equal to the love you make."

Chris

What I've Learned

I have learned so many valuable lessons through Scott's life and death. The most important one that I hope to share with parents who have not lost a child is the importance of spending time together. In the end, the only 'thing' children want from their parents is their time. Physical possessions like iPads and cell phones were not part of Scott's memories. Experiences together as a family riding bikes, hiking, and playing board games, those are the memories he cherished. Enjoy your children, for they truly are a gift from God. I have also learned that love has many layers. Of course, you love your family and friends, but when your child is facing death, you love so much deeper. Scott's illness and death were not about me. I had to put my feelings aside and make sure he was all right. To let him go peacefully, with his questions answered, his worries eased, were the hardest things I ever had to do. I never knew I was capable of such love. If I can do this, you can too. We are moms. I've learned that death is not a final goodbye. I know Scott is watching over me and I live each day trying to make him proud. I know that I will see him again and when I do, I want him to say, "You did good, Mom."

During the writing of this book, many people asked me if I thought it was cathartic. At first my answer would have been a very loud, "Hell no! No, it was not." Many times, the memories would leave me ugly, crying, sobbing as I wrote. However, as the final ending came into place, I am acknowledging how amazing this journey has been. I feel from every fiber of my being that I was meant to tell this story which has deepened my faith and given me strength, peace and so much love and joy. As I wrote, I was amazed at how clearly I saw God's hand throughout my life. He certainly has a plan for me. I remember shouting to the sky, "Are you there Scott? Are you happy? Do you miss me?" The signs I have shared tell me that he is there and he does miss me. The signs have strengthened my bond with Scott and with God. He has a plan for everyone; you just have to keep your eyes open and it will reveal itself and it will be amazing. I am so grateful for this experience and really believe that Scott is more than okay, that he continues to make the world a better place.

As I reflected on my worst-case scenarios, I realized that this was always when my faith was tested the most. These were such low moments that I honestly did not know if I would survive. As time passed, though, I can clearly see how each of these scenarios turned into best case scenarios. Yes, I was a single mother, then Gene and I found love again, rebuilt our family and our lives, ultimately finding true happiness and joy. We can still laugh – Best Case Scenario.

Yes, our son died. He lived three and a half years with his illness, a year and a half beyond all expectations. We are so grateful for that time, love and those precious memories. From the pain of losing Scott, I was chosen to write this book by God and Scott. I got to work with my deceased son and I am forever grateful to have felt his presence, his love, his encouragement, and his guidance. How many people can say that? Definitely, Best Case Scenario.

Also, those Beatle lyrics Scott so loved" Let it Be", "Take a sad song and make it better", "And in the end the love you take is equal to the love you make" were far more than just a song. They were a lesson for life.

On April 30, 2011, Scott's family and friends gathered at Hitchcock to celebrate his life. The eulogy was offered by Scott's cousin Mike:

For those of you who do not know me, I am Scott McMurray's cousin. Over the years I have come to learn that he was one of my greatest strengths. Whenever someone found out that we were related, they'd invariably say, "Wow, Scott's awesome, you're so lucky," or "he's the funniest kid I know." I think I went up a few notches in their eyes just by association. Scott had the ability to make friends without even trying. People gravitated towards him. He could move from one group to another and fit in seamlessly. Looking around this room today, that much is very clear. Scott was a great person who impacted the lives of many that he met.

Over the last few weeks I have been thinking what I would remember the most about Scott. I can say without hesitation that he is the funniest person that I've ever met as well as the most fearless. Sometimes I feel I am not as upset as I should be knowing that he's gone, but it is impossible to think about Scott without smiling. The legend of Scott has many chapters. There was the time he decided that running for school president just wasn't good enough ...so he ran for king of the world. I have no doubt that if anyone was actually running against him, he'd have won in a landslide. Scott has always said that he invented the word guacamole. I cannot verify this, but I have no reason not to believe him.

We took a vacation upstate a while back. Scott was probably about seven years old. Aunt Chris always wanted us to be outside, so we went hiking one day. It became clear pretty quickly that this wasn't the best idea! I looked over the edge of a cliff and nearly passed out. Kim nearly slipped off a rock and into the river below. At this point it was unclear if we were going to make it off the mountain. Then there was Scott, jumping from rock to rock with a big grin on his face, surely wondering what was wrong with the rest of us.

Another memorable story that stands out occurred on a family vacation that we took to the Outer Banks about eight years ago. I remember pulling up to the house, there were balconies on the second and third floors overlooking a pool in the back. I believe the first thing our parents said when we arrived was, "guys, do not jump off the balcony and into the pool, we don't want anyone to get hurt." Most of us thought that was a reasonable request. Not Scott. He took it as a challenge.

So one night all of the cousins are in the pool fooling around when we see Scott come out of the house and over the railing. Now, this wouldn't be a Scott story if he just jumped and was done with it. Scott had a flair for the dramatic. He decided to combine his daredevilry with a stand-up comedy routine. He would jump and in midair began doing impressions of everybody in the family, one by one. Uncle Eugene for his voice cracking when he gets annoyed. Aunt Barbara for the smoking habit she has since kicked. My brother Jim for truly believing that he is the smartest person on the face of the earth. On and on it went, we loved every minute of it!

Scott had the unique ability to make jokes or pranks at your expense and have you laughing right along with him. Even towards the end, he never lost his sense of humor. When we found out a few weeks ago that the end was near, the thing that hurt the most was thinking about the dinners and holidays we will be spending together five, ten, twenty years from now without Scott being there. Then I realized I was wrong, Scott did not leave us empty handed. We will always cherish our time with him, those stories and how he made us laugh. His family and friends will be telling these tales for the rest of our lives. We still have the inspiration that he gave us in his last days. The most important thing that Scott has taught me and I'm sure, many of you, is never stop living, never stop laughing, because they go hand in hand and you never know what lurks around the corner. No one lived a fuller twenty-two years than Scott McMurray. There was a quote that Scott posted on Facebook just a few weeks ago. Winston Churchill said, "I am prepared to meet my Maker. Whether my Maker is prepared for the great ordeal of meeting me is another matter." Scott, I love you and I'll miss you, but try to go easy on everyone up there.

We all have special memories of Scott, here are a few –
From Aunt Eileen –

My nephew Scott, was an extraordinary person. From the beginning he had a twinkle in his eye, a knowing smile and a zest for life. Being his quiet, reserved aunt, I greatly admired and envied these qualities in him. He always made me chuckle. Just the mention of his name brought up an image of one of his many antics. He, my niece Kim, and my four children spent countless hours together – sleepovers, Friday pizza nights, holidays and summer vacations. Scott was always the comedian. His pranks and stories were very creative and displayed how very clever he was in a way that can't be measured. As he grew older, his many friends experienced this same spirit. He just had a knack for living life to the fullest and sharing his joy with everyone around him. When Scott was diagnosed, he demonstrated even more character, yet he stayed the same. His bravery and determination were a source of great pride to his family. He fought a battle that gave us all inspiration to live our lives as he did. Despite his pain and struggle, he still had dreams and plans for new adventures. My nephew taught me so much before and after his illness. Although our pain in losing Scott is great, the joy he gave us and his example to love and live life to the fullest, is an incredible gift that lives in our hearts forever.

From Kathryn –

There's a picture of Scott and I when we were little that depicts our relationship perfectly. He was about two years old, sitting in a high chair. I'm about six, sitting on a picnic bench next to him. We're both laughing, my arm around his shoulders looking out into the distance. It makes me smile every time I see it because it reminds me of his laugh and how he always seemed to make me laugh too.

Scott was four years younger than me, but when we'd play games with our cousins, Kim and Mike usually wanted to be on the same team. So, then it was always Scott and me. Sometimes having a four-year-old as your partner was a disadvantage, especially during a scavenger hunt when he couldn't read the clues. But secretly, or maybe not so secretly, I was always happy I had Scott on my team. I was a bossy kid, but Scott was able to handle me with a smile, a joke or a teasing "come on Kathryn, let's just play."

Looking back, I realize that what most drew me to Scott was that somehow I always knew he loved me just as I was. I didn't need to be more easygoing, funnier or cooler. That was the thing about Scott – if he liked you or loved you, you knew it and he didn't need you to be anything more or less. That's not easy to find, even in the best people. Scott loved with his whole heart. He was also the bravest person I know. I used to think he was fearless, but I don't think any of us are without fear. He just knew that life was too big and beautiful of an adventure to let fear stop him. There are many things I want to tell him, but I also know he's with me every time I'm scared or taking things too seriously. In those moments, I can almost hear him laughing, reminding me to loosen up and just play.

From Megan –

I've looked up to Scott ever since I can remember, but it wasn't until I started middle school that I realized my admiration was shared by pretty much everyone else he'd ever met.

Scott was two years ahead of me, an eighth grader, and the most popular kid in school. Everyone knew his name and his class clown antics were already legendary. All of the girls had a crush on him (a girl in my class somehow got her hands on an 8x10 photo of him and hung it in her locker). I was amazed. In sixth grade I was half the size of everyone else, was painfully shy outside of my family and small circle of friends. Middle school was a pretty scary place for me, but from where I stood, Scott had it all figured out. It sounds ridiculous now, but by absolutely no fault of his own, I was intimidated and scared of cramping his style. Looking back, I wish I had followed his lead and spent less time being afraid.

At some point that year, I signed up to perform a solo at my chorus concert. The day of the concert I was so overwhelmed with stage fright that I begged my teacher to let me off the hook. She said no. I stood trembling on stage and looked around for my mom and siblings for reassurance and saw Scott sitting with them. He had heard about my solo from Aunt Chris and Uncle Eugene and even though they couldn't make it, he took it upon himself to find a ride from a friend. He had been looking right at me and when he caught my eye, he started making silly faces. I laughed and for a few seconds just before it was time for my line from "Colors of the Wind," I felt too happy and special to remember how scared I was.

When I think about Scott, this story always comes to mind and makes me smile. I think it explains two of the things that made me and everyone else admire him so much. First, he had figured out that there was nothing in life so scary that it couldn't be confronted with a good laugh. And when he loved you, he showed up for you, even if it meant sitting through a bunch of eleven year old's singing a medley from Pocahontas off key!

From Aunt Barbara

As the last to add my two cents, I wondered what I could say about Scott that has not already been said by his parents, his sister, his cousins and his aunt. I have many memories of Scott that point out all of the wonderful qualities that made him the special person he was. He did have the devil in him and that glint of a smile always reminds me of the weekend I was staying with he and Kim and he was picked up for tossing Styrofoam off the roof of the Galleria parking lot. Somehow, he managed to keep that under wraps until his parents returned. He was the leader of the pack and during our 'Aunt Barbara weekends' he could always be counted on to come up with entertainment options that included everyone. Scott was the skateboard king of White Plains and I am amazed that this hasn't been mentioned before. One afternoon I was driving down South Broadway in White Plains business district and saw this young man. probably about 12 or 13 years old, come flying down the steps of an office building on a skateboard, only to land smoothly, pick up his board and went back to do it again! Upon closer inspection, guess who!! Needless to say, he didn't find my warning to be careful and less of a daredevil was warranted.

I remember a special nod of approval I got one Christmas when he opened a gift I wasn't too sure was his style. That little nod of the head told me I had nailed it. But more than anything, I remember his kindness, his loyalty, and the way he showed everyone in his world how much he loved them. There is no question in my mind that Scott was the best friend one could have and his friends knew it. Since he has passed, more young men than I can count have come up to us and identified themselves as Scott's best friend. He had a way of making everyone feel special.

Scott left behind lessons for all of us. Some were learned during his too short life. Many others have come to us in the years since and for me especially, as I have helped his mom during the writing of this book. This was an honor for me, not only to participate in this special work, but also to get to know this special nephew of mine just a little better and to learn from his acceptance, courage and willingness to embrace the hardest of all – the unknown. Maybe now, through his messages, we can look forward to that unknown with greater faith and hope that someday we will all be together again.

From Jim

For my family and so many others, my cousin Scott was the comet that flashed across our sky. Brilliant and bold and fearless, he always blazed his own path and seemed to do it at ten-thousand miles an hour. As we watched, he left us all in awe of his humor, intelligence, kindness, and courage. And then he flew away much too soon. But when he left us we were grateful that we got to be a part of someone so special and unique. We knew that many people never get to see a Scott fly across their sky, and we knew that we would never know anyone like him again.

A lot of times when I think of Scott, it really is a memory of him almost literally flying. Some of the stories have been ably described by my brother Mike—like the time that Scott, barely older than a toddler, zoomed past us down a waterfall, jumping from slippery rock to slippery rock, as the rest of us inched downward holding on for dear life. He was my little cousin, but he was the leader I needed to get me to the bottom of the mountain that day.

Or the time Scott predictably defied his parents' orders not to jump from the third-floor deck of our beach house into the pool below. What was not predictable was that Scott would combine his aerial acrobatics with simultaneous, spot-on imitations of everyone in our family. I'm not sure there is anyone in the universe with the creativity to combine comedy and death-defying stunts into a performance like Scott did that day. I don't think I've ever been better entertained.

And then there was the time we all went to see a Broadway show. Scott was in the middle of his battle with cancer, but cancer could not stop Scott from being Scott. As we were filing down the stairs to exit the theater, there was a flash across my field of vision—not unlike a young child jumping down a waterfall or a comedian diving down three stories into a swimming pool. This time it was Scott sliding all the way down the bannister in the middle of the stairwell and executing a perfect landing on the floor below. As Scott waited nonchalantly for us to catch up with him, I laughed to myself about how that stunt must have shocked and dismayed some of the theater types. But I also laughed in amazement at the spirit inside of Scott that allowed him to live his life like that, even as cancer tried to take it away. Scott was like a comet in so many ways, but unlike a comet, he never burned out. He was Scott until the very end.

Stories like this are just a few examples of who Scott was and why I admired him so much. That admiration caused me to take great pride in something as little as Scott calling me to ask for a ride home after some teenage mischief got him and his friends kicked out of the local amusement park. Scott might not have given it a second thought, but for me it was an honor that he knew he could count on me for help if he needed it.

The last time I saw Scott may have been the saddest day of my life. But it also may have been the most important. That day, I got one last chance to look at him and tell him that I love him. He told me the same. To this day, it is hard to believe that was the last time I saw Scott and that he isn't with us anymore. The realization can hit me out of nowhere like a ton of bricks. But even when I feel sad remembering that he isn't here, I also remember how thankful I am for the happiness that Scott brought to all of us, and how lucky we were to watch him fly.

From Kim:

When Scott was dying, really, truly dying, I used to read to him from a book called Physics of the Future. He would lay in bed with his eyes closed and listen to me read about space elevators, rescue robots, and molecular medicine. I paused when my throat got too scratchy or tears threatened to spill down my face (I was always on the verge of crying those weeks), and Scott would say, "keep going," or "just a little longer," or "how much longer do you think until robots rise up against us?" Sometimes we would talk about the ideas in the book, but mostly I would read and he would dream about a world that he would never get to see.

When I think about those last few weeks, I think about that book.

Scott died on a Wednesday morning. My dad was the one to tell me but I knew as soon as I heard him coming upstairs towards my room. I kissed him good-bye, and when the undertaker came, I was scared that my mom wouldn't let go. But she did and we sat at our dining room table so we wouldn't have to see them take his body.

The next few days are a blur. I remember we sat on the porch a lot, breathing slowly and greeting the steady stream of family, friends and neighbors. I remember so much food. Brownies from my college roommate. Fried chicken from my aunt's best friend. Strawberries, scones, and short ribs.

My aunts and my cousins were permanently at our house, and at some point we made collages for the wake. Photos of Scott smiling, healthy, and in midair.

I remember my poor jalopy of a car stopped about three blocks from our house when I ran out to run an errand, and never turned on again.

I remember zipping my black dress and applying mascara for the funeral. I remember walking into the church and standing when you are supposed to stand, and then not being able to stand anymore. And taking my heels off and drinking a glass of red wine on the receiving line.

But mostly I remember not remembering. Because for the first few seconds of each morning, for the first few days, my brother wasn't dead yet. He was just downstairs waiting for me to read about avatars.

I still keep the book on my bookshelf. It has made every move with me from Philadelphia, to DC, to New Hampshire, to Vermont, and back to DC. I don't think I will ever finish it.

My favorite memory of my brother is the time we had a water gun fight in our kitchen, but instead of water, we used ketchup, pickle juice, Kool-Aid and anything else we had in the pantry. Why did we do this? I don't know except that Mom wasn't home and Scott suggested it. So Scott, and two of our friends, and I filled our water guns with chocolate sauce, built barricades out of kitchen chairs, and declared war.

See, Scott was fun. He was so much fun. But as his older and more serious sister, I wasn't always in on the game. Like when he gave tours of my room to his friends, including my diary and my underwear drawer. Or when I had friends over and he would prank call them from the phone line in my room.

One time, the summer after I graduated high school, I was walking up to the house as Scott and his friends were leaving. It was after dark and I was looking forward to a night sprawled out on the couch watching tv. "Hey Kim," Scott said, "we are going to go play ring and run. Want to come?"

I scoffed. "No way!" I was far too mature to ring someone's bell and then hide behind their hedges when they answered the door.

"Come on! It will be fun!"

But still, I demurred. And Scott and his friends scrambled off to trick some unsuspecting neighbors. Honestly, I still don't get the point of ring and run. So someone answers their door and they are a little confused? Big deal.

Still, I really wish I had said yes.

Live, Laugh, FLY!!

Afterword

Gene and I decided to end this book with an update on our lives.

It has been eight years since Scott has passed and we feel we are finally coming out of a long tunnel. We will always miss Scott but we know without a doubt, that he is with us, he is happy and pain free. We continue to see signs but at this time I do not plan on writing a sequel.

We are living in South Carolina and doing our best. I volunteer with Meals on Wheels and I am also taking care of children for several families. This brings me so much joy and I love when they ask me to tell them a 'Scott Story.' Gene is scaling back on work and improving his golf game. He is active in his twelve step program, together we enjoy traveling, the beach, family and friends. Kim lives and works in Washington DC and is engaged to a wonderful man named Scott. How cool is this? We get to say Kim and Scott again! Another sign?